Hollyfield

– DAVID FORWARD –

An environmentally friendly book printed and bound in England by
www.printondemand-worldwide.com

This book is made entirely of chain-of-custody materials

www.fast-print.net/store.php

Hollyfield
Copyright © David Forward 2011

All rights reserved

No part of this book may be reproduced in any form by photocopying or any electronic or mechanical means, including information storage or retrieval systems, without permission in writing from both the copyright owner and the publisher of the book

ISBN 978-184426-993-8

First published 2011 by
FASTPRINT PUBLISHING
Peterborough, England.

This book is dedicated to all the pupils, staff, parents, governors and supporters of Surbiton Central School and its successor, Hollyfield School.
Since 1938, at two different sites in Surbiton, they have worked to create and maintain an outstanding school and to ensure that education really does make a difference

.

The author joined the teaching staff at Hollyfield in 1979 and was deputy headteacher, including a period as acting headteacher, from 1985 until his retirement in 2009. This book was written in gratitude for a successful and rewarding career.

Hollyfield:
The history of Surbiton Central School 1937 – 1966 and Hollyfield School, Surbiton 1966 - 2010

Contents

Surbiton Central School, Hollyfield Road 1937 - 1966
- The Holly Field and early education in Surbiton
- Planning for a new school
- The start of Surbiton Central School 1937 - 1939 Major FWC Hill
- The war years 1939-1945 Lt. Col. FWC Hill
- The post-war period 1945-1956 Lt. Col. FWC Hill
- The final decade at Hollyfield Road 1956-1966 Mr Olsen Humphreys

The move from Hollyfield Road
- The relocation to Surbiton Hill 1966 Mr Olsen Humphreys

Hollyfield School, Surbiton Hill Road 1966 - 2010
- The new Hollyfield 1967-1972 Mr Olsen Humphreys
- The flat period 1972-1976 Mr Annets
- A new energy 1977-1985 Mr Iowerth Harries
- The pastoral years 1985-1993 Mrs Eileen Serbutt
- Becoming an outstanding school 1994 - Mr Stephen Chamberlain

Pupil memories

Other historical links to Hollyfield
- The history of Albury House
- Surbiton County Grammar School
- Hollyfield and St Mark's Church

A chronology of events 1937 – 2010

Famous staff

Famous pupils

The punishment book

Lists - Headteachers
- Deputy headteachers
- Long serving teachers
- School Plays
- Certificate evening speakers
- School inspections
- Pupils who have represented their country
- Head Boys
- Head Girls

Bibliography

David Forward

Surbiton Central School, Hollyfield Road 1937 – 1966

The Holly Field and Early Education in Surbiton

The Holly Field existed in the mid 19th century bordering a hill on the Ewell Road which led from Kingston, with its bridge over the Thames, through Tolworth village and on between fields to Ewell village and the south. At the time there were several farms in the vicinity with corn being harvested annually. The areas of Kingston, Surbiton and Tolworth as well as Malden, Chessington, Hook and Coombe were then all in Surrey. There were no state funded schools in Surbiton or Tolworth although nearby Kingston had a Grammar School established by a charter of Queen Elizabeth 1 in 1561. In the 17th century the Tiffin Schools were also established in Kingston to enable "honest poor men's sons" to be taught to "read, write and cast accompt". Other local schools recorded in Kingston were a Sunday School, opened in 1798 in Brick Lane, now Union Street, and a Ragged School, built in Old Bridge Street in 1853 for the very poor children of the back lanes.

During this era, Surbiton was very much a village based rural community with only a few houses, many of them ramshackle, with muddy tracks connecting to Kingston, Tolworth and Thames Ditton. The area only started to develop its own significant identity when the railway came in 1838. At this time the Surbiton station area was called "Kingston on Railway" and remained so until the Kingston line and Kingston Station opened in 1863. The opening of the railway started a period of rapid growth for the Surbiton area including the construction of the large private dwelling of Albury House and its stables and grounds in 1856, currently still a focal point of The Hollyfield School.

In the 19th century many new schools started opening up in the Kingston, Surbiton area. Many of them had church sponsorship and in 1876 attendance became compulsory and school attendance officers were sent out daily to catch truants. The 1902 Education Act allowed Kingston and Surrey to establish Education Committees and new schools appeared. These included a variety of Elementary Schools and in 1921 the school leaving age was raised from 12 to 14 years of age making the Elementary Schools bigger. In the Surbiton and Tolworth area these included Tolworth Central School, Christ Church - Church of England School, and St Andrews Road Church of England School. This is confirmed by the Surbiton Hill Handicraft Centre log book which is held as part of the Kingston archives. Based at 35 Ewell Road, the Handicraft Centre, consisting of one main classroom, opened in September 1910 and served these schools on a weekly timetabled basis for practical craft work until 1937.

Planning for a New School

A new school was needed as many of the local farms had been sold off to building developers and the population of Surbiton and particularly the part of it known as Berrylands, was growing rapidly. The site chosen, was on King Charles Road, between the stream which leads to the Hogsmill River and the country lane opposite the Fishponds. Alexandra Park was being developed on the other side of King Charles Road. This would have been a prime site in an attractive largely open area and was where the main school building was purpose built during 1936 and the early part of 1937. Hollyfield Road, previously a cul-de-sac into the Holly Field off the main Ewell Road, was extended early in 1937. This replaced the country lane and formed a proper road link between the Ewell Road and King Charles Road at a cost of £1200. To prevent any subsequent encroachment, the Fishponds area opposite the front of the school was designated as permanent open space.

David Forward

The country lane by the Holly Field with the new school under construction 1936
Source: Surrey Comet

The construction of Surbiton Central Mixed School 1936
Source: Surrey Comet

Hollyfield

The prestigious new Surbiton Central School, built facing the new part of Hollyfield Road, was the beginning of what was later to become The Hollyfield School. It was to be on that site for twenty nine years until 1966 when it would move about a mile to the north, up past Berrylands and over the Waterloo to Surbiton and Portsmouth railway line to its current location on Surbiton Hill.

Surbiton Central School viewed from the new Hollyfield Road 1938
Source: Kingston Museum & Heritage Service

When the Surbiton Central School site was vacated in 1966 it subsequently became used for Adult Education and in-service teacher training courses and educational administration. It changed its name to the King Charles Centre and is still in similar use by the Kingston upon Thames Education Department.

The start of Surbiton Central School 1937-1939 (Major FWC Hill)

Surbiton Central School in Hollyfield Road, first opened its doors to pupils on 24 May 1937. It was formed from the amalgamation of three smaller schools; Tolworth Central School, St Mark's Church of England School and Christ Church, Church of England School. The first headmaster, Major FWC Hill OBE TD, initially oversaw 352 pupils (185 girls and 167 boys) and 11 staff. Major Hill was assisted by a "Chief Woman Assistant" Miss M.E Guyer, who taught domestic science.

David Forward

The old Surbiton Central Mixed School site in 2010. It is now the King Charles Centre used by Kingston upon Thames Local Education Authority for administration, training courses adult education classes.

The Surrey County Council log book, held as part of the archives of the current The Hollyfield School, shows that most of the staff had either teaching certificates or academic degrees with two having MA's. The school opened with one overseas teacher, a Miss Simon from South Africa and its first supply teacher was a Mr Evans, who covered for Mr Watson, who was taking his BSc finals.

The original staff list as in the school log-book:
  Headmaster Major FWC Hill
  Chief Woman Asst. Miss ME Guyer
Assistant Teachers:
  a) Permanent Appts.
      Mr EV Bull
      Mr EH Hillman
      Mr J Kenyon
      Mr FC Peacock
      Mr SWB Watson
      Miss L Reeve
      Miss LP Watling

b) Attached Teachers
   Mr FA Lamb
   Miss Gabbott
   Miss Simon
c) Supply Teachers
   Mr Evans
   Mr JG Lang
   Miss McHardy

It is interesting to note that the male teachers were listed before the female teachers.

At its inception, the school was run under the aegis of Surrey County Council's Education Committee as it was well before the formation of the London Boroughs which did not occur until 1965. It was designated as Surrey Council School number 332. The official opening of the new school took place almost two months after its actual start when on 12 July 1937 the Mayor of Surbiton, Alderman W Sanger attended the ceremony which included a service, speeches and tours of the building. It must have been a very exciting time for the pupils and staff taking possession of their brand new school particularly as there had been so much publicity generated locally.

From the time of its 1937 opening Surbiton Central School also managed the premises at 35, Ewell Road as an arts annex. It had closed as a designated handicraft centre two weeks before the Surbiton Central School opened and the Surbiton Central School's official log has several references to lessons in it throughout the 1930s and 1940s with pupils walking up there on a daily basis. Although relatively insignificant to begin with, this annex was later to become a base for one of the school's most successful courses and some of its most famous pupils.

The first school trip was to the Odeon cinema on 20 January 1938, when, according to the log record, the whole school went to see a series of health films arranged by the County Council. It is pleasing to note that this initial positive attitude regarding the value of trips and visits to education has continued on throughout the life of the school.

The school log reveals that Major Hill was a keen member of the Territorial Army and that this required occasional days off to attend functions and army training. However, this did not appear to prevent the school from making a successful start as an inspection in March 1939 recorded: "This school, which is still in its formative period, has made an admirable start. Boys and girls from different schools are working together well....". The inspection also commended the opening worship of the day, the very well thought out schemes of work and the school's sound ideas concerning the Bible. The staff were described as "able and keen".

It is clear from the comments of ex-pupils and staff, that for the majority, Major Hill was a popular headmaster. He was well known for patrolling the school to ensure good order amongst the pupils and for supporting his staff. He was described as a well dressed, slim and short man who was very capable of "addressing his troops" with a powerful voice when necessary.

The War Years 1939–1945 (Lt. Col. FWC Hill and Others)

During the second World War, the school buildings were undamaged. However, conscription affected the school when the headmaster, now Lieutenant Colonel Hill, was called up on 25 August 1939 to lead the 67th Anti-Tank Battalion of the Royal Artillery. This is poignantly recorded in the school log in his own handwriting and unusually in blue ink; "I have been mobilised as Commanding Officer of 67th anti-tank Regt. RA. FWC Hill – Lt Col. RA." During his absence a Mr FW Beale was temporary headmaster from September 1939 to September 1942 after which Mr Hill returned for one term until the 31 December 1942 when he was called up again, this time to command the 96 Anti-Tank Regiment, RA. If he had suffered the fate of "the many" then this would have been his last entry in the log but fortunately he returned to the school on 20 August 1945 when the log states; "I have returned to take charge of the school again having been away in the Army". A Mr H Cleland was the temporary headmaster from 11 January 1943 but, upon the final return of Mr Hill, he returned to Cheam County Secondary School.

During the war, air raids were frequent. When the "alert" sounded the school evacuated across the road to the nearby trenches and their shelters where a roll was immediately taken and lessons of one form or another continued as much as possible. Should a whole school evacuation not be deemed the safest option, possibly because bombing had already begun, then a bell was rung by the headmaster and pupils remained in the main building. Staff absence due to illness at this time was high and sometimes the reasons for absence included having to deal with air raid damage in their own houses or attending war related courses such as "Emergency Cooking" or accompanying groups of evacuees down to Devon. Many staff were moved about or seconded to local and more distant schools. Empire Day was enthusiastically celebrated with amended timetables, talks and "appropriate songs" in the morning and then a half day holiday. Diseases such as scarlet fever became more frequently reported at this time.

The war time difficulties of the school can be felt in this section of the log book written by Miss Guyer who was acting up for the temporary headmaster, Mr Cleland, as he had been injured in a bombing raid: "During the week ending June 23 work has been carried on principally in or outside the trenches. All children attending have been issued with a note-book and an emergency syllabus has been arranged. We tried working in school at first, between "Alerts", but on two occasions we were only just able to get to the trenches before the bombs were heard, and so many journeys were made that it was decided that more work would be done by staying near the trenches."

Attendances were in single figures on some days during 1944 in particular, due to the disruption caused by the bombings. During the night of 22-23 June, 123 panes of glass were broken by blast damage as well as there being significant door damage. In one week at the end of September 215 panes and window frames were repaired.

Mr Cleland returned to duty as temporary Headteacher on 16 October after his blast injuries and following a further few difficult months the staff and pupils were able to celebrate Victory Day with the nation for which the school was officially closed on both 8 and 9 May 1945. Lieutenant Colonel Hill returned to the school from active service on 20 August 1945 and then served continuously as headmaster after the war until his retirement in 1956.

The Post-War Period 1945–1956 (Lt. Col. FWC Hill)

The after war years were hectic with a lot of teacher movement and pupil activities. It must have been very helpful to the school to have such a constant figurehead as Mr Hill during this time.

Shortages affected the school, for example, in the extreme winter of 1947 the 35 Ewell Road classroom froze in February and was closed for a while as was the school itself for two weeks of the following month when stocks of fuel ran out. The school log records; "Stocks of fuel have been exhausted and there is no heat in the school at all. On the advice of the Divisional Executive Officer, school has been temporarily closed as from the afternoon session until a supply of coke is obtained. Children will report to school on Monday, Wednesday and Friday mornings for instructions. Timetables of work have been arranged whereby children will have some work to do at home and activities such as Handicraft, Domestic Science and Physical Training will be carried out at school. Mid-day meals and milk will be provided for those children whose parents desire them to have it at school during the emergency. Educational visits will be arranged if a prolonged closure is likely."

Managing the school even after the war must have been quite difficult for Lt-Col Hill as pupils steadily left the school during the year, some to the grammar schools at 13+ and others moving away from the area. In addition to having the new GCE exams to administer he also had to manage a steady stream of staff changes as well as frequent supply staff to cover staff illnesses and training courses. He worked well with his staff and also made a good impression on new staff, for example in 1947 when interviewing Joan Randall as a new needlework and domestic science teacher as he revealed an interest in sewing and that he had made himself a pair of trousers!

Ex-staff report that they always referred to him formally as Lt-Col and that he had the gift of discipline in that he was a kindly and fatherly figure who naturally commanded respect. He would regularly walk around the school, known as "showing the flag" and have a look in classrooms. Gordon Eke (1947 -1951) describes Lt-Col. Hill from a pupil point of view as "not a very big man in stature but a one for imposing his authority, I think he treated his school as an extension to his army career. He was also very good with a thin bamboo cane, knew exactly the right place to inflict the most pain."

He appears to have been ably assisted by his deputy, Miss Mabel Guyer, known to the girls as "Fanny Guyer", but regarded as a strong disciplinarian and who taught cookery, housewifery and needlework, and subsequently by Miss Nora Byrne, later to become deputy headmistress, who taught PE and dance. Notable, during this time, were the very popular dance displays organised by Miss Byrne. Not only did she attract a lot of visitors to her dance shows but the teamwork helped to generate a happy atmosphere amongst the girls as the older girls were apparently always very good at helping with the younger ones. The "Demonstration Dance Team" was a very skilled and well known group within the school during Miss Byrne's time, as well as also holding a wide reputation outside the school. Members of the dance team spent many hours in school rehearsing for the performances as well as much time at home sewing ribbons onto skirts in preparation. One of the abiding memories of various members of the team over the years was that Miss Byrne always looked old, the grey hair probably aiding this view and even more memorable, that she wore a short gym slip and used to keep her handkerchief up her knicker leg!

The summer saw many activities taking place out of doors including the Sports Day at the Alexandra Recreation Ground opposite the school. Houses were used as the basis for sports and in 1949, Tennyson House won the boys' trophy and Faraday House the girls' trophy. The first swimming gala was held at the Surbiton Lagoon in 1953 and swimming, led by Mr RG Davies, became quite popular with creditable performances in the annual District Gala and events such as the life-saving club being attended at Kingston Baths. Accompanying the emphasis on swimming the school had a motto: "Every boy and girl a swimmer".

Sports reported in the school magazine include netball, football, rounders, cricket, swimming, athletics and boxing. Other activities include orchestra, violin and recorder clubs, choir, drama and a very popular ballroom dancing club. In 1952 the ballroom dancing class after school was so popular that its 100+ members had to be divided up. The school magazine, which had a section on ballroom dancing written by the teacher George Mellon-Grant, records; "the first half-hour of each evening was allocated as a beginners only class, being followed by a period of dancing interspersed with the introduction of old-time and novelty dances". It also adds a piece of advice to any reluctant pupils: "Forget your shyness; don't wait to be chased on the floor each time a dance is announced; the more effort you put into it the quicker you will learn and really enjoy ballroom dancing."

In addition to these activities and clubs the school log reveals a remarkable range of trips and visits including the first ever school trip abroad to Belgium, also in 1953, which was repeated for several years. Also at this time, amidst much excitement, was the coronation of Queen Elizabeth II. On 2 June 1953, Mr Morman and Miss Derbyshire took 28 pupils to see the coronation procession to Westminster of the soon to be Queen Elizabeth II, part of a group of 30,000 school pupils given viewing places on the Victoria Embankment. On the 18 June the whole school went to see the coronation film "A Queen is Crowned" at the Surbiton Odeon Cinema. In addition, Surrey County Council gave the school a grant of £10 to purchase an object or objects associated with the coronation. Following a consultation by the headmaster the school bought a lectern bible bound in maroon leather and embossed with the school crest in gold. The senior woodwork class made a lectern out of oak wood for it.

The facilities at the school annex at 35, Ewell Road, usually just referred to as "35", were causing concern. However, radical change was planned as the school log records that in 1950 the headmaster was involved in meetings with His Majesty's Inspectors and subsequently the Clerk of Works, about improving the facilities there and for a new art course to run there for pupils selected on the basis of their talent, some of which would come from other schools at 13+. The improvements were made and the new art group thrived and continued to attract pupils from a wide area around. Ably taught by Mr RC Dyson, the Art group regularly obtained a pass rate of 100% at GCE. Several pupils from this group every year went on to Kingston School of Art and indeed, it was this route that was followed by many, including Eric Clapton, in the years ahead.

In the main school building at Hollyfield Road, another highly regarded course was Miss Randall's Commercial class, whose girls also regularly obtained good results as well as typing up the school magazine and programmes for events such as Prize Day.

The Surbiton County Secondary School magazine "Hollyfield" produced its inaugural edition in 1950. Its editor for many years was Mr FA Lamb and the cover was usually screen printed by members of the art group from 35. The printing was also done by the Art Department using a heavy duty silk screen printer which later moved up with the school to the Surbiton Hill Road site where it did many more years service before being relegated to the corridor outside the art rooms in Hill House before being scrapped in the late 1990s. Perhaps because of the greater art influence in the curriculum and the successes of Miss Byrne's dance performances, school plays and concerts were also developing into more professional shows. The 1950s Christmas concerts were no exception and William Wilcox (1956 – 1958) remembers the "Junior Art", as the 35 group were known, working on quite complex scenery and prop projects.

School trips also continued unabated and in those less politically correct days Bryn Town (1953 – 1958) remembers a trip to Bristol to visit the W.D. & H.O. Wills' cigarette factory and also the Fry's chocolate factory. He also remembers going as part of a school group to Ireland with the headmaster and deputy head and staying at Skerries near Dublin. Even though it was a trip abroad, the pupils had to wear school uniform including the usual maroon blazers when they were out although apparently not all the pupils wore their caps and berets.

A school trip to Ireland in 1955 with Mr Bullivant (far left) Miss Byrne and Lt-Col Hill (far right) and pupil Bryn Town (far right back row).
Source: Bryn Town

In the 1955 magazine, the year before Mr FWC Hill retired, the staff were listed as:

Mr F.W.C Hill OBE, TD, Headmaster
Miss N Byrne, Deputy Head

Miss PJ Barnett	Mr RG Davies
Miss HM Derbyshire	MR RC Dyson, ATD, DA (Manc.)
Mrs KM Foley	Mr HJ Grant, BA
Mrs G Geall	Mr FA Lamb, BA
Mrs PM Hancock	Mr S McGinn
Miss PW Hodge	Mr G Mellon-Grant
Mrs EM Jarvis	Mr RCS Raine
Miss JM Randall	Mr FF Rooks
Mr R Allen	Mr CE Roos
Mr MA Attewell, BA	Mr AT Storey, FRGS

Mr RJ Bullivant   Mr PJL Strachan, ATC
Mr PJ Coote, ARCM, LTCL Mr J Williams

Note that the female staff are listed first this time but only the male staff have their qualifications shown. The only member of the support staff listed was Mrs D.G.J. Head, the headmaster's secretary although Mrs Watkins (canteen) and Mr Gould (Caretaker) do get a mention and thanks in the headmasters report. The headmasters report was rounded off with an exhortation to pupils to "See that your conduct both in and out of school, and your enthusiasm for work and games are such that you maintain the good name of the school, and in doing so prepare yourself to become worthy citizens of your Borough, County and Country." Nothing much changes!

As the inaugural headmaster who held post for almost 20 years, F.W.C. Hill, working within the constraints and opportunities provided by the Surrey Education Committee, must be credited with shaping the early form of what would later become The Hollyfield School. His career, although punctuated by two spells of "war leave" and holding considerable challenges in developing the school after the war, can only be regarded as pioneering and very successful. Without doubt and with a clear focus he managed this non-military command with effective leadership based on mutual respect, a focussed vision of the value of education and a clear determination to make the school and its pupils successful. In his school log entry on the penultimate day of term before his retirement at the end of August 1956, Lieutenant Colonel F.W.C. Hill wrote that he would "always look back over my years here since 1937 when I opened the school with great pleasure and memories of a very happy and loyal school". The school should regard him forever as its foundation, as its father figure and as a true educational pioneer who imprinted Hollyfield solidly on the educational map.

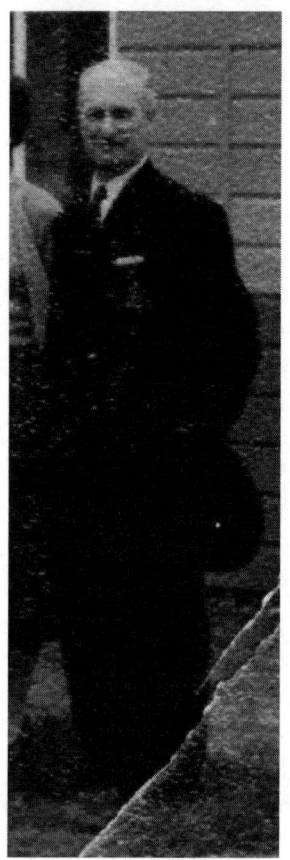

Lt – Col FWC Hill in 1955
Source: Bryn Town

The final decade at Hollyfield Road 1956–1966 (Mr Olsen Humphreys)

Lt. Col. Hill was replaced as headmaster in September 1956 by Mr Olsen Charles Humphreys, previously the headmaster of Western County Boys' School in Mitcham. In an interview for the school magazine, Mr Humphreys described his own school days as beginning in 1910 at the "Tankerton College for the Sons of Gentlemen" where pupils did not have pens or paper readily available but had to write with chalk on slates instead. He was later awarded a BA Honours degree in history at London University before his post-graduate training as a teacher of history. In September 1931 he was appointed to the Adams Grammar School in Newport, from which he moved in 1938 to Epsom

County School. After service in the RAF during World War 2, during which he attained the rank of Squadron Leader, he returned to Epsom County before obtaining his first headship at Western County Boys' School in 1951 and then moving to Surbiton County Mixed School in Hollyfield Road in 1956. Olsen Humphreys lived in the family home in Epsom, so it was a relatively easy journey for him each day.

In a later interview by the school magazine, he commented that the educational pressures on young people seemed a lot less in his early headship days. However he noted one exception to this which was the Matriculation Exam. This examination, taken at the end of a pupil's school career, required a pass in every subject to obtain the certificate. It was critical, as if just one subject was not passed then the whole examination was failed.

Olsen Humphreys
Source: Maureen Humphreys

When the 1944 Education Act was enacted the school was formally classified as a "Secondary Modern" and therefore lost several pupils each year to the more prestigious "Grammar Schools" as they topped up their numbers. This amounted to 15 pupils in 1952 with a further 6 being lost later in the same year after being successful in the 13 plus selection examination which was in effect a second chance 11 plus. This constant creaming off of the more able would have been disappointing to Olsen Humphreys as well as disruptive to the school as classes would have to be more frequently adjusted. It also required a different type of curriculum which was supplied by a range of technical and commercial courses.

Sports, including the boxing managed by Mr Mellon-Grant and also music seemed to be thriving throughout this era with many references to them in the school magazine ably edited by the English teacher, Mr Lamb. The drama club was thriving, although the "Hollyfield" magazine commented that more boys were needed! The ballroom dancing club was still very popular and had over a hundred members on several occasions. The dance group run by Miss Byrne also continued its popularity and maintained its excellent reputation and was frequently required to put on performances for other schools and for local events.

The Dance Group with Miss Byrne in 1957 after it had put on a display of "Continental Dancing" at Grand Avenue Primary School Fair. Sarah Solly is front left - Diana Turner is to the left of Miss Byrne.
Source: Sarah Solly

The school log shows that Mr Humphreys had quite a baptism of fire in his new post. In 1956 he began the term with 168 new pupils and was then disadvantaged by needing an acting deputy head for a week due to illness and also soon lost a member of staff who resigned after a nervous breakdown. Unfortunately, OC Humphreys was not such a great keeper of the school log as FWC Hill, his predecessor and in the October after his appointment his comments reduce to phrases and then end completely at the start of November 1956. It picks up again with the same hand, three years later, in September 1959 which writes to the end of November when it is completed in a completely different hand but with brief references to key events until March 1964 with one last comment ending 28 years of the handwritten school log, added by Brigadier Butters, Chairman of the Governors under Surrey County Council who wrote "Change over to Kingston on Thames Royal Borough."

Despite its relative sparseness, the log clearly shows a degree of frustration by Mr Humphreys, particularly when his competence was tested. For example in September 1959 he wrote "Miss Gibbs, HMI, spent five hours cross examining the headmaster on the finer points of education in this school with special reference to internal examinations."

As the school continued to grow, two moveable classrooms were added in 1959. These were placed at the back of the main building and required the filling in of the school pond. There were bicycle sheds and separate playgrounds for girls and boys. A favourite activity in the boys' playground was watching out for sports cars from Cooper's Garage on the corner of Hollyfield and Ewell Roads. The mechanics often used to drive fast up and back Hollyfield Road, showing off to the admiring pupils as they used the road as a test track. The interest would have been even greater after 1958 when Stirling Moss won the Argentine Grand Prix in a Cooper Climax. Some pupils used to walk past the garage every day and one, Peter Dilloway (1958-1963) once saw Bruce Mclaren there and after speaking to him was given a ride with him in a British Racing Green coloured E-type Jaguar. Jack Brabham, Stirling Moss and other Grand Prix winners were also seen at the garage. Outside the garage were parked the cars that in addition to Cooper racing cars and Jaguars included exotic cars such as Railton, Bugatti and Lagonda – a boys dream and a frequent topic of playground conversation. The mini-cooper car was built and tested there before its launch in 1961. Another pupil, Roger Hunt (1962-1964) was an avid observer and claims that he can still hear them as they pushed the cars down the road to get them started!

In the autumn term 1959, the school was gripped by a court case pertaining to the murder of the father of Roger Purdy, one of its pupils.

Roger's father was Detective Sargeant Raymond William Purdy of the Metropolitan Police who came to national attention when he was shot through the heart whilst on duty. The fatal shot was fired from a semi-automatic pistol by Guenther Podola, a German born criminal, during a police chase and arrest in South Kensington. The court case rapidly followed and Podola was sentenced to death. He was hanged and buried in Wandsworth Prison and was the last man to be hanged in Britain for killing a police officer. His trial was made the more controversial because of his defence of amnesia and the use of expert witnesses to determine whether his illness was real. Pupils were often in conversation as they avidly exchanged views about reports from the newspapers on the case and its subsequent dramatic result.

Another event remembered by many of the pupils was the annual ripening of the crab apples on the trees in front of the school by the Hollyfield Road fence. This invariably led to crab apple fights in the boy's playground. Another playground favourite occurred in the summer months when an ice cream van was allowed to park in the girl's playground at the end of school. This was very popular with the pupils although I doubt that Miss Byrne was so enamoured as she took on the responsibility of managing the queue.

Hollyfield teachers on a school trip to Weggis in Switzerland circa 1958-60. Miss P J Barnett (RE), Mr A C Hann (mathematics), Mrs Hann and Mr Hockey (geography). Source: Michael Ferris.

David Forward

The boys of classes 5A and 5B in the girls' playground with Mr Mellon-Grant 1961/2. Back Row:Left to right: Graham Cryer. Trevor Teasdale. Alan Williams. D.McMahan. Dave Taylor. Mike Martin. Chris Box. David Holland. Roland Ell. Christopher Butler. Brian Orys. Derek Lowden. Chris Thain. Middle Row :- G Gallagah. Alan Searle. P Bain. G. Sands. William Randles. John Wren. Keith Turner. Hans Grey. John Humphrey. Graham Nash. D Green. Front Row:- R Parks. Harish Surtani. M Cutts. A Mason. Mr Mellon - Grant (Form Teacher). Terence Earny. Robert Anderson. Dave Benson. A Jarvis.
Source: Brian Orys

The school continued to have an active and varied extra-curricular programme. This included large scale play productions such as Jane Eyre in 1960 using the Hall stage and its sound and lighting equipment. The1962-63 edition of "Hollyfield" contains many such reports on events including House Plays, the Christmas concert with the choir, dancing and drama groups participating and the annual speech day held at the Kingston Coronation Baths Hall. The dancing society continued its popularity and high reputataion under the command of Miss Byrne, the Christmas skiing trip was to Austria and the Easter tour was to Belgium, Luxembourg, Germany and Holland. These "extra" activities did much to maintain the dynamic ethos of the school and for many pupils they are still fondly remembered as excellent, sometimes life-long relationships were built up not only between pupils, but also with the staff.

Jane Eyre 1960 with Frederick Wakefield (Lord Ingram), Rosemary Caspell (Lady Ingram) and Ann Bryant (Mrs Fairfax)
Source: Surrey Comet

Another big talking point was in 1963, when a fire, allegedly started by an unhappy pupil Ian ("Inky") Gordon, gutted the school hall which was also used as the gym. Inky, according to some of his peers, was an intelligent boy but rather hyper-active and a fidget so no one who wanted to work liked to sit next to him in class. His nickname derived from his rather messy use of his Osmoroid pen which resulted in him always having inky fingers. Although it is thought that he did not act completely on his own Ian apparently bought paraffin from the corner shop opposite and entered the school one weekend through a window of the hall that he had secretly left slightly ajar. He is thought to have spread the paraffin around the hall, then entered the adjacent science labs and turned on all the gas taps, set alight to the paraffin and left. This created quite an inferno and with the possible ignition of gas would have been potentially catastrophic. However, the fire brigade arrived promptly and whilst they were not able to save the hall, the science labs were largely saved.

Damage to the Hall from the 1963 fire.
Source: Hollyfield archives

There is not much record of the fire or the repair work which followed although George Mellon-Grant, the teacher who had taken over leadership of the popular boxing club which used the hall, wrote in the school magazine about "the complete destruction of the ring, ropes and canvas" and that the teams would have to "box away for some considerable time". Linda Parfitt (1962 – 1969) was a pupil during this time and as a PE hater was initially full of joy that the hall/gym was out of use but soon regretted it as without the gym most of the PE had to be done outdoors instead!

Geoffrey Miller (1959 -1964) was also pupil at the school when the fire occurred and confirms that it was mainly the school hall that was damaged. He remembers when:

"Chris Melrose and myself turned up for school as usual on the morning after the fire and walked past the front of the hall on Hollyfield Road to reach the boys' entrance gate. The first indications we saw were that various windows had burst and there were burn and scorch marks around the paint work areas. The actual main structure of the building appeared to be totally intact." He also remembers Mr Rook, the physics teacher, being extremely upset because all the lighting equipment that he had built up for the stage was totally destroyed. He also says that the outer shell of the hall was basically sound and was quickly patched and cleaned up and some activities were then carried on in it and he still has a memory of the permeating smell of the burnt wet wood and images of the puddles of molten glass.

Activities such as morning assemblies were moved to the British Legion Hall just down Hollyfield Road which was already being used for school dinners and some assemblies, whilst the full hall refurbishment was done during the summer school holidays. Marian Gordon, who was one of the Art teachers, remembers that Ian Gordon wrote to Mr Humphreys from prison and apologised for the fire. Mr Humphreys, demonstrating compassion, subsequently asked the staff not to hold any further negative feelings towards the boy as he was doing his punishment and had apologised.

Although the brevity and incompleteness of the school log gives little away, it is clear that Olsen Humphreys had a real heart for children. A variety of activities and events occurred including the Headmaster's "At Home", an after-school meeting with staff and prefects for a short informal tea. Staff relate that he invariably got on well with people with his free and easy manner and that he was always full of ideas. However, he was apparently not as good at "showing the flag" by walking around the school or as strong a disciplinarian as his predecessor. Many ex-pupils particularly remember his "Oh, Oh, Oh, Oh" laugh and most remember his mortar board and cane. Stephanie Carney was a pupil at that time and had a lot of respect for the headmaster's leadership: "During the Friday all school assembly he taught us to be honest, look people in the eye, have a firm hand shake and above all to have courage and guts! If one of us behaved badly outside the school we let the whole school down. Simple, but important values."

Another pupil who remembers Olsen Humphreys well was Audrey Whyman (1959 – 1963). She found him approachable, fair and with a good sense of humour and describes an example: "…when he came walking along a corridor where I was standing outside my classroom door. I thought I was really for it now – he asked me why I was there and I explained that I had got the giggles when Mr Grant (history) was explaining about the army of Poles marching across the fields, and I had been sent out of the room. Mr Humphreys gave a slight smile and simply said, 'that sounds about right' and walked on! "

Peter Lawson (1959 – 1965) also remembers Mr Humphreys as a strong but fair disciplinarian. When Peter attended the school the "teddy boy" era was in full swing and knuckle dusters and chains were sometimes seen and boys hair with a quaff and side-burns with a boston or a duck cut was very fashionable. Peter was once "slippered" by Olsen Humphreys for defacing an exercise book by drawing teddy boy pictures in the margin. He also recalls that Mr Humphreys would tweak the side-burns of any boy who had grown them to excess, and lift them gradually until they were standing on tip-toe. Then, he would warn them to reduce it and occasionally would actually give them the money to get a hair cut. Peter says that it usually worked!

Peter Leckstein, a pupil from 1959 – 1963, describes Olsen Humphreys as "a man of vision, determined to enable all pupils to achieve their potential." He adds that this was particularly important as many pupils felt cheated by their failure to pass the 11-plus exam. Peter was in the first cohort of pupils to take the new "O" level subject examinations in 1963 which replaced the increasingly disliked Matriculation examination. Peter also remembers the fogs or smogs that used to engulf the school during November and December. He describes the fogs as thick dense and choking which sometimes necessitated that the school finished early in order for pupils to be able to get home safely. The buses were frequently reduced to a crawl and the school, being next to the open spaces of the Alexandra Recreation Fields, seemed to suffer particularly badly.

Other teachers in addition to Mr Olsen Humphreys and Miss Nora Byrne ("Nobby"or to others "Bandy") at that time remembered by ex-pupils, included Mr George Mellon–Grant who taught chemistry and did boxing; Mrs Bradley, music; Mrs Geall and Mr Hann, maths; Mr Grant ("Grandpa"), history; Mr Gealy, woodwork; Mr Williams ("Taffy"), technical drawing and metalwork; Mr Rooks ("Ronnie"), physics; Mr Kedge and Miss Derbyshire, English. Miss Derbyshire apparently later became Mrs Rudge when she married a widowed parent of a pupil from the school.

Memories of these teachers include that Mr Williams was well known for his accuracy with pieces of wood which were sometimes thrown across the metalwork room to attract the attention of boys at the back. Mr Rookes was known for his high domed head and Mr Grant for his ability to see good in almost everyone. One of the most memorable quotations of useless information remembered by many boys over the years is one from Mr Gealy, the woodwork teacher; "the hardest softwoods are sometimes harder than the softest hardwoods"!

Rosalyn (nee Allen) (1958 – 63) and Graham Whitfield (1962 -66), two ex-pupils who later married, also remember the staff well. Between them they recall that Mr Humphreys, the headmaster, was a nice man who seemed to them to be very fair. Miss Byrne was the deputy head for the girls and also took Rosalyn for P.E. Miss Dawe taught English. Mr. Davies taught history and could lose his temper. Mrs Kinstrie taught maths and religious knowledge. She had blonde hair and a gold tooth and was a fearsome character so all the girls used to call her "Cruella", especially after she hit a pupil on the back of the head! Mrs Mcquillan taught both cookery and sewing. The sewing room was in the main building and cookery was done in the annexe across Hollyfield Road. Rosalyn describes Mrs Barretto as "a lovely lady" who taught her maths.

Graham also remembers many of his teachers from that era including Mr Gealy who he thought was a fearsome woodwork teacher. He describes how one day Mr Gealy told the class to sit still while he went over to see the Headmaster (the woodwork room was in the annex across the road.) When he came back he thought he knew that someone had moved. He picked out three people, took them into the back and caned them. However, it turned out that he was caning a brown paper covered stool which gave the other pupils the impression that he was caning. Mr Cunningham taught Graham PE and Mrs Bradley, taught him music with the class often taking advantage of her as she did not control them. It seems that she once had a nervous breakdown in front of the class which Graham says was very sad and shocking and he still remembers it to this day. Mr Kedge took him for English and gave a lot of spelling tests. Mr Farr took metalwork in the huts across Hollyfield Road, but this was not Graham's favourite class. Mr Lamb was a small grey haired man and many pupils were in fear of him not least because he used to walk into the classroom to cane a boy and the child was allowed to choose which cane he wanted to be caned with!

Pupils at the time were often playing tricks on the teachers. One famous incident was the construction of a "pipe-bomb" using phosphorus stolen from George Mellon-Grant's chemistry laboratory together with icing sugar. It was sealed with a glow plug from an engine from metalwork, put in a pipe and buried in the ground in the

Fishponds area opposite the main building. It was connected by a length of fuse wire to a battery in one of the desks in Miss Bradley's music room hut which was also on the Fishponds side of the road. After much nervousness it was eventually set off and caused quite a loud explosion, enough to cause Mrs Bradley to scream and also to bring out the police and fire brigade. The culprits kept a very low profile.

Another favourite activity of some of the pupils, to annoy teachers such as Mrs Bradley, was to buy sherbert dips from the corner shop and to blow through them to make a cloud of sherbert and make it look like they were smoking in class. This would have been quite a tease as Mrs Bradley was a heavy smoker and even smoked in front of pupils during after school music practices and rehearsals. Apparently, her fingers were so nicotine stained that they were almost the same colour as the opal ring she wore. On another occasion a class member carefully bored a small hole in a piece of chalk in Mr Gealy's woodwork room and put a "Swan Vesta" match in it. When Mr Gealy wrote on the board it caught fire and burned his fingers. He apparently leaped over the teacher's bench and ran into Mr William's room next door shouting at the top of his voice. The whole class was punished. Another incident once led to the evacuation of the whole school. This was the result of some pupils misbehaving during lunch time in the physics laboratory during which a bunch of keys was thrown which unfortunately broke the large pane of protective glass at the front of the fume cupboard. The enveloping smell was horrendous and safety required all pupils to remain outside for a considerable time which soon caused the incident to be regretted by all concerned.

The art group continued at 35, Ewell Road, known to the pupils as "35" with pupils joining it at 13+ and then having most of their lessons there. Generally the other pupils found the art group to be a rather insular and aloof but it was obviously an incredibly dynamic group as it formed the school's first debating society in 1962 and its first film society the following year. This class was a prestigious one for the school and attracted some excellent teachers including, during the late 50s and early 60s, the popular Mr Dyson and Mr Strachan. The location on the Ewell Road was between the church and the fire station so was often referred to by the pupils as being between heaven and hell!

35 Ewell Road in 2010 – converted to an architect's office.

Christine Windon was one of the "35" pupils and remembers that whilst she seemed to be constantly walking from Hollyfield Road up to the art block next to the fire station in Ewell Road, this provided lots of opportunity for wasting time! She describes Mr Dyson as a very laid back head of art whose pupils were much envied by those back at school who had to tow a more academic line. The upstairs of "35" was relatively formally set up with easels for painting whilst downstairs was used for crafts, including ceramics, which could be fired in the kiln. Pupils who went to saturday art classes there also remember the nude female model – quite an eye opener in those days!

It was this art group that Eric Clapton joined in 1958, travelling in daily along the railway line from Surrey. He was thought to be moody but there were reasons for this linked to his home experiences. Pupils did enjoy his concerts in the Hollyfield Road school hall and also impromptu events at "35" particularly at lunch times with others such as Chris Dreja and Anthony Topham with all three subsequently going on to play in the Yardbirds and then having largely separate but very successful musical careers. The new English version of the American Rhythm and Blues which they played and which transformed the popular music of the early 1960s was born out of Hollyfield and from these three Hollyfield pupils who strummed in the 35 Ewell Road cloakroom during lunch times.

Peter Lawson (1959 – 1965), who was also in the art group remembers Eric, Chris and "Top" well. Eric was sometimes to be seen staring into the windows of the Bell Music shop in the Ewell Road. Peter remembers him with his nose right up to the glass looking at a beautiful cherry red Burns electric guitar. His own guitar was more of a cello like acoustic guitar with an arch top. It was painted gloss black and Eric had painted white around the sound hole and the f-holes. Chris Dreja used to go to Peter's house sometimes for lunch and either play guitar or listen to records and was also the first of their peers to have a motor bike, which was greatly admired. Peter also remembers with horror the day that "Top" came into school with a radically changed hair style. Gone was the trendy long hair and quiff, instead he had a crew cut which made him the laughing stock of the boys at that time.

Eric moved on to Art College in 1961 but was persuaded to leave after a year as he was spending more time on his music than his art work. Christine Windon remembers that Eric used to come back to school sometimes during this year to practice in their form-room with his friends who were still at the school. After art college he replaced one of his Hollyfield friends, Chris Dreja, in the Yardbirds when they went professional and by using the new fashion of electric guitars contributed to a whole new dimension of rock and pop music. Eric next played in Cream and, despite several personal difficulties, gradually became known as one of the greatest rock musicians of all time. He was recognised for this and received the CBE from the Princess Royal at Buckingham Palace and in 2006 received the Grammy Lifetime Achievement Award. (See section on famous pupils for more information)

Another person, soon to become famous, joined the school in 1960. Anne Wood was an English teacher and continued as such until 1965 when she left teaching to work as a publisher and later as a broadcaster and philanthropist. She was clearly dynamic, setting up a book club and producing school plays and many pupils were inspired by her teaching of English and English literature. She later achieved fame and wealth as the author of the televised childrens' series the Teletubbies. (See section on famous staff for more information).

The Young Visitor – House Play 1962 – produced by Anne Wood. The page boys on the right were Robert Warrior and David Moss-Bowpitt. Christopher Wren is in the striped jacket. Source: David Moss-Bowpitt

The choir and orchestra 1965 – Miss Bradley is in the middle and far left holding the drumsticks is Nigel Treherne who became a well known oboist and composer. Source: David Moss-Bowpitt

Music and dance continued to be a significant part of the school's life. In 1965 Miss Bradley was in her last year as music teacher at the school and was replaced by Miss Bentley with Mr Knight and Mr Impey taking most of the instrumental lessons. A particularly exciting event took place in October 1965 when, after weeks of practice, the choir and orchestra performed a recording for the BBC. It was made the more exciting because the pupils were transported to and from White City by BBC coaches and because they saw several celebrities whilst they were rehearsing and recording.

Mysteriously the name of the school appears to be poorly defined at this time. It seems that the name of the school drifted from being Surbiton Central School at its inauguration to Surbiton County Secondary School as in the 1955 magazine. Futuristically, the 1955 magazine was called "Hollyfield" and in it one of the contributors Mr PJ Coote, the music teacher, despite the clear heading of "Surbiton County Secondary School", refers to the school as "Hollyfield". The first reference in the school log to the name of the school being Hollyfield was in the entry dated 4 October 1960 when the school was referred to as Hollyfield County Secondary.

The Move from Hollyfield Road 1966

The re-location to Surbiton Hill 1966 (Mr Olsen Humphreys)

During the headship of Olsen Humphreys one of the most significant events in the history of the school occurred – the move up to the Surbiton Hill Road site. This major event occurred soon after 1965 when Kingston became an education authority in its own right.

The school had well over a year of preparation for the move and this affected the school community in different ways. Firstly, the school play, The Gondoliers directed by Mr Davies, was the last in the old school hall and was seen as a finale which required a massive effort which impacted on much of the work of the school from September 1964 to its performance in March 1965. Also, the PTA had tried to arrange the last summer fair before the move, up at the new school on Surbiton Hill, but the site was not ready in time.

The new site at Surbiton Hill had previously been used by Surbiton Grammar School, a boys' school and so the facilities, particularly those for girls, were initially poor. This meant that for some lessons in technical subjects, pupils had to return to the old site in Hollyfield Road and some teachers, including Mr John Williams (Taffy) the metalwork teacher who was in charge, Miss Gordon (art) and Mr Gealy (woodwork) stayed there for another year or two. The headmaster used to telephone down regularly to the old site to check with Mr Williams that everything was in good order. Apparently, he once heard children laughing in the background during one of these phone calls and demanded a reassurance from Mr Williams that all was as it should be.

The Gondoliers – the last play at Hollyfield Road.
On the left is John Pilkington (The Duke), Judith Bidmead (The Duchess),
Kathleen Clunie (Casilda) and David Moss-Bowpitt (Attendant).
Source: David Moss-Bowpitt

This was a temporary situation which, along with the continuation of some lessons at 35 Ewell Road, awaited the construction of the new art and technology block, to be named Hill House after the previous headmaster, at the back of the Stables block up at Surbiton Hill. When this was completed, all the staff were together on one site and the new Hollyfield School was at last able to establish itself fully. In the 1966/67 school magazine, Olsen Humphreys refers to the new site appreciatively:
"…..the graciousness of Albury House, the spaciousness of the classroom block of Villiers, the excellent gymnasium, and the community atmosphere of the new domestic science block."
Staff who transferred from Hollyfield Road up to Surbiton Hill with the school have fond memories of the cosiness of the old school. Miss Gordon (art) felt it was a more personal place because it was small and Mr Gealy (woodwork) described the original school as "a big family" rather than a large organisation.

Hollyfield

*Albury House as it would have looked soon after the new school started.
Source: Dan Leissner*

However, he bemoaned the damage that the overcrowded pupils were doing to property and also the gradual decline in the relationship between pupils and teachers because of the increase in numbers.

A pupil who remembers the move well was David Moss-Bowpitt. He writes from Ireland:

"My first recollection of the move from Hollyfield Road to the new buildings in 1966 was that they were not ready for the whole school at the start of the year. The exam years were allowed in and we were taught in various rooms that were ready. All the other age groups were sent home for an extra week of holiday. Even then there were builders and decorators about for the first part of the year.

Like many, my daily journey to school was lengthened and it took me some time to adjust to leaving home earlier and not being able to pop back home at lunchtime. As I lived in Tolworth on the far side of the A3, the journey was increased by about a mile.

Our links with the 'old site' were not completely severed. The new buildings did not contain woodwork/metalwork/technical drawing workshops as these were not taught at Surbiton Grammar School so we had to make our own way back down to the old Hollyfield Road site for these subjects. My over riding memory of the change of site was suddenly having space all around us, a hall large enough for the whole school to meet in, gardens with green space, a few mobile classrooms and an on-site dining hall.

As a keen sportsman one of the great improvements the move of site afforded us was the improvement in the sporting facilities owned by the school. At the old site we only had the small school hall to use indoors and the Recreation Ground opposite where we largely used the small field nearest the school. A cross-country run meant a trip round the local streets. Once we moved we inherited the pitches at Hook and although this again meant a trip, when we got there we had full pitches for football, rugby and cricket as well as plenty of space for athletics. On the school site there was the much improved indoor space in the gym and space outside for courts in the playground, cricket nets and grass space for badminton courts in the summer.

The classroom facilities were also much improved by the move. I remember the feeling of much more space and lighter classrooms. The science laboratories were much improved and there was the old building which gave the school a great deal more character than at the old site. Later in that first year the Prefects Room was set up above the stable area and this was seen as a terrific facility for the senior years in the school. It really came into its own after the exams. In those days there was no study leave even when exams had finished but as we had no lessons to go to the recreational facilities were well used and the 'Sergeant Pepper' Album hardly ever off the record player. I also remember that we were all employed in various jobs round the school including knocking down some old garages and building partitions in some rooms to create office spaces and cupboards."

David later became a teacher and concludes by saying: "I have many other fond memories of the school and have always been grateful for the start it gave me and most particularly the motivation and confidence to go to make the most of any ability I had. I feel that I was able to call on the values I learnt at Hollyfield throughout my career in teaching and the school was central in helping achieve what I have."

Beverley Whitehorn (now Swain) (1964 -1969) was a pupil who attended both sites and remembers the move as "an amazingly smooth transition (for the pupils at least)!"

She says: "I went home after completing my second year at Hollyfield Road in July '66 and started my third year at the new site in

September. It felt like we'd been there forever and it seemed huge in comparison. Another thing was that we were allowed to mix with the boys! At the old site, we had separate playgrounds and staircases and only saw the boys in class and the regular whole school assemblies. It was lovely to have so much space and grass - it was like being at school in the middle of a park. We had proper classrooms and science labs - even one of those new fangled language labs! The only negative was that we had to get a coach to the field whereas at the old site we walked over the road to Alexandra Recreation Ground."

Beverley does not remember seeing much of the Heads at the old site but when the school moved to Surbiton Hill she says that they appeared to be around much more and had quite an 'open door' system. She remembers that Miss Byrne was always known by the pupils as the "headmistress" rather than the "deputy head" as she dealt with the girls and Mr Humphreys sorted out the boys. Beverley recalls Miss Byrne as "a real Miss Brodie type ….a very straight laced spinster". She taught biology as well as PE and dance and Beverley remembers it was hilarious when the topic was reproduction and says: "We had the usual lecture on ' when a man and a woman love each other they get married, then and only then they………' She was very stern and strict, expecting us all to be well educated young ladies. When a girl in my class became pregnant at barely 16, we all feared the worst! The whole year group of girls were taken into the hall (without the girl in question) for what we thought was going to be a lecture on the outcomes of loose morals. What we got was the most understanding, sensitive and caring talk from a woman who visibly softened before our very eyes - a golden moment and one I cherish." Beverley continued to be a significant part of the history of the school herself as in 2003 she joined the staff as a teaching assistant forming part of the select group of people who have been both pupils and staff.

David Forward

Hollyfield School, Surbiton Hill Road 1966–2010

The New Hollyfield 1967 – 1972 (Mr Olsen Humphreys)

The move and the building work that was still going on made Hollyfield seem more like a brand new school to the majority of pupils. Villiers (now Sharman House) was only two years old and the new art and technology block was under construction. The new school was spacious and green. The staff in 1967-68 were:

        Headmaster: Mr OC Humphreys
        Deputy Head: Miss N Byrne
        Senior Master: Mr HJ Grant

Mrs WA Barretto	Miss B Symons
Mrs J Bayliss	Mrs LF Taylor
Mrs J Burridge	Mrs S Tamblyn
Mrs JJ Caminer	Mr PG Clarke
Mrs W Clarke	Mr CR Day
Mrs PA Davies	Mr RC Dyson
Miss R Dawe	Mr SG Finklestone
Miss M Gordon	Mr PJ Fuller
Mrs AM Horne	Mr GC Gealy
Mrs C Knight	Mr AC Hann
Mrs JA Kinistrie	Mr DH Kedge
Mrs A Lalor	Mr G Mellon-Grant
Mrs P Murray	Mr OG Requena

Miss JM Randall	Mr FF Rooks
Mrs CE Ransom	Mr LMP Swanson
Miss JM Roberts	Mr P Thorning
Mrs HM Rudge	Mr J Williams

The school secretary/bursar was Mrs Joan Jecock who replaced Mrs DGJ Head, known to the pupils as "Headie", who had worked at the school from the early days of the war when she joined the canteen staff at Hollyfield Road as "meals secretary" and worked as school secretary to Mr Hill as well as to Mr Humphreys. She was well known to all the pupils and a lynch pin of the school on both sites but unfortunately died in September 1968 just after her retirement. This would have been another blow for Olsen Humphreys as his own wife Rosina had died in 1967.

Olsen Humphreys outside Albury House
Source: Surrey Comet

The school uniform was burgundy skirt for the girls and grey flannel trousers for the boys, burgundy pullover, blazer and beret for the girls and cap for the boys. Girls report feeling so much more grown up when they went into the 3rd year (now year 9) because they could ditch the pleated skirt for a straight one and the yellow and burgundy tie was changed for one that had blue stripes as well and the beret was never seen again!

Pupils attending the school at this time also generally liked it although not all were so impressed with some of the attitudes of Mr Humphreys and his deputy, Miss Byrne. One pupil who moved south and joined the school late with a northern working class background found it hard to be accepted, particularly by the senior staff. Initially, she was not allowed to become a prefect or to read out loud in morning assembly although this was apparently rescinded later.

One of the things that many pupils really appreciated about the new school was that the canteen gave them a choice of things to eat for lunch, much better than the British Legion Hall canteen in Hollyfield Road. There was also the popular tuck shop run from the double doors half way down on the inside of the Hall.

Olsen Humphreys worked hard to give the new school a high profile locally. One of his early coups was to arrange for Dame Sybil Thorndike to give the prizes at the 1967 Prize Giving. This annual event was held at the Coronation Halls in Kingston and required that the swimming pool was covered over so that temporary seating could be installed. Although Prize Day gave Mr Humphreys a good platform through which to give positive messages about Hollyfield to the press, dignitaries and parents, it was unfortunately a very noisy venue and pupils soon found that banging on the floor made quite a disruptive noise! It was this that later led to the use of the Surbiton Assembly rooms as the prize giving venue.

Many pupils also appreciated that trips and visits continued to be given a high priority, a tradition that has remained an outstanding characteristic of the school. Also the House system continued strongly with Raeburn house colour being red; Faraday, yellow; Elgar blue and Tennyson, green. Houses were used for sports, music and dance competitions.

As the curriculum expanded a range of both CSE (Certificate of Secondary Education) and GCE (General Certificate in Education) subjects were offered.

Despite the school continuing to lose its brighter pupils to the

David Moss-Bowpitt with Dame Sybil Thorndike on Prize Day 1967
Source :David Moss-Bowpitt

Grammar Schools, Mr Humphreys remained strongly against the ideals and practices of the comprehensive system and supported the 11 plus examination system as he thought that trying to make everyone equal was an impossible ideal. He said: "Over the years, the secondary schools have been gradually working up to the standards of the grammar schools, and this is the way the system should work." He was also a staunch supporter of co-educational education stating: "Boys and girls together is the right way to have a school."

Olsen Humphreys continued to be a popular and well respected headmaster but rumours started circulating in 1969 when he was seen with a much younger teacher from another school. The rumours were transformed into great excitement when it was announced that he would be remarrying. He had met a PE teacher, Elizabeth Drake, from nearby Tiffin's Grammar School on an educational cruise in the Baltic Sea and they were married on 20 December in Beckenham, Kent.

*The Prize Giving 1969 at Surbiton Assembly Rooms.
Pupils including Josephine Langhorne, Christine Dagless, Susan
Boxall and Kathy Clunie are performing a folk song.
Source: Christine Ensor*

The pupil gossip was all the greater because he was 63 and she was 29 years old, two years younger than Olsen's own daughter Maureen. The school choir were taken over to Beckenham and sang and formed a guard of honour at the wedding. The couple continued to live at the family home in Epsom and soon their daughter Deborah was born.

Olsen Humphreys retired when he was 65 in the summer of 1972. Although not as long serving as his predecessor Major FWC Hill, he of all the headteachers of Hollyfield probably did more to shape the school and set it up for the next phase of its history. He certainly commanded more press coverage than most headteachers and was vociferous in his pride for the school and in support of his staff and pupils.

Reflecting on this, when the Surrey Comet interviewed him on his retirement he said "In the last 16 years, Hollyfield has progressed from a small secondary school with very few pupils staying on beyond the statutory age, to what is virtually a comprehensive school." He also confirmed that his idea was always to "educate the whole person" and to make all pupils a "part of the community".

Olsen and Elizabeth on their wedding day in 1969
Source: Surrey Comet

Olsen Humphreys in a relaxed mood.
Source: Maureen Humphreys

Soon after his retirement aged 65 in 1972 he was presented with an illuminated certificate for long service by the mayor, Councillor Claude Potts. The mayor congratulated him for doing such a good job as headmaster of Hollyfield. Reflecting on his strongly pastoral style Olsen described the trend of large schools which cater for 1000 or more pupils as a "curse of modern education". Despite this I suspect that he would have some admiration for the current 1100 pupil Hollyfield which was built on his foundations with its strong pastoral care and good academic achievement. Olsen House, built when the school leaving age was raised to 16 in 1973 was so called as a tribute to him. He visited the school for functions several times after his retirement and lived a long life until his death on 27 February 2005, aged 98.

The Flat Period 1972-1976 (Mr Annets)

Mr Annets replaced Olsen Humphreys and was headmaster from 1972 – 1976. He wore the traditional flowing black academic gown and was clearly a disciplinarian as evidenced by his frequent of use of corporal punishment. Staff found him to be rather different to his friendly predecessor as he adopted a more formal ethos and tried to move the school back to what he perceived it once was. It would seem that he was generally on good terms with most of the staff but perhaps not with as many pupils. The punishment book, started in September 1972, was headed "Punishment Book, Mr Annets" and always kept this heading even though it covered the period right through Mr Harries headship and up to its last entry in May 1986 when Mrs Serbutt was the acting headteacher. Mr Annets travelled in from St Albans each day which must have been quite tiring.

*Looking up towards Villiers (later renamed Sharman) block 1973.
Source: Dan Leissner*

An innovation during the time of Mr Annets was the presence in the school of the Department for Hearing Impaired Children (DHIC). Although looked after by the unit staff, hearing impaired pupils were fully integrated into the school and carried a radio transmitter which complemented one worn by the teacher. It was very important for the teacher to be aware that even if they left the classroom they could still be heard by the pupil. Several teachers, for example in Science, have spoken to a technician in an adjacent preparation room and said something that caused the hearing impaired pupil to be in a state of great hilarity when they returned. Generally the hearing impaired pupils did well and were a well respected part of the school.

Pupils and staff who had experienced the more liberal ways of Olsen Humphreys found Mr Annets harder to deal with. He was known for making up his own mind rather than consulting and was not as well regarded by the pupils perhaps because of his strictness which was hard for some to cope with. During this time pupils were strictly streamed as classes A – D within the school and the maroon blazer, jumper and for girls, skirts were worn until the fourth year when a black blazer was worn. Girls wore skirts, never trousers.

The site was very much open to the outside with little low walls where they did exist so it was easy for pupils to escape. Pupils frequently used to be found on the bank on Surbiton Hill, now the raised flower bed near the traffic lights, or on the corner of Cranes Park.

Sadly, very little documentation remains from this period of the school's history. Clearly it would have been hard for anyone to have replaced the charismatic Olsen Humphreys, but Mr Annets' strong disciplinary line and his attempted return to traditional values at a time when young people were rebelling through different styles of dress and appearance and when drugs were becoming more available was always going to be a hard line to take. Mr Annets does not appear to have captured the imagination of either pupils or staff. He maintained his social distance from both, an example of which is that no-one of his era appears to even know his first name. It is also not on record why he left or what he did subsequently. Following the departure of Mr Annets in 1976, Mrs Joyce Culver was temporarily promoted to acting head for the Autumn term. She had previously joined Hollyfield in 1970 from Tiffin Girls' School. Those who knew her described her as a kindly woman who was a great help to young teachers and very fond of cats.

Hollyfield

The school from the crossroads in 1973. The Villiers block towers over the canteen and gymnasium roofs.
Source: Dan Leissner

The Villiers block viewed from the Lamberts Road entrance 1973
Source: Dan Leissner

An even greater sadness occurred when she died a year later in November 1977 aged only 49, apparently after being taken ill whilst attending church one Sunday evening. This was a big shock as things appeared to be normal and the previous Friday she had been working in school late preparing for the forthcoming annual Christmas Fair. A memorial service for her was held on 24 November at St Mark's Church. The school was closed for the day both out of respect and also because most of the staff and many pupils wished to be in attendance at the service.

A New Energy 1977-1985 (Mr Iowerth Harries)

In 1977, Mr Iowerth Harries commenced work as Hollyfield's fourth substantive headteacher following the short period of "acting up" by Mrs Culver. Mr Harries was interviewed by students Ian Lord and Sharon Rock, in September 1979 for the inaugural issue of Hollyvine, the new school magazine, which was published the following month. This reveals that he was from a family of teachers and was educated at a mixed grammar school in Cardiff where he decided also to join the teaching profession. He taught first at a secondary modern school in Wood Green followed by a spell at Elliot Comprehensive School in Putney. He was then promoted to the post of deputy headmaster at a school in Blackheath. His appointment as Hollyfield's fourth headmaster was his first headship.

In his Hollyvine interview he specified his objectives as improvement to the library and public relations especially through advertising the school's "O" and "A" level examination results. He was concerned about spending cuts in education and saw himself working closely with the Hollyfield School Association (HAS) and the old students organisation to raise money for improvements to the school.

Iowerth Harries in his office 1979
Source:Hollyvine Magazine

Mr Harries was subsequently interviewed, again for Hollyvine, by a student, Mark Belchamber, in 1982. This confirmed that he was born in Cardiff and that he was brought up as strict baptist but professed to be "somewhere between baptist and loose agnostic". He had previously taught in a secondary modern, a grammar and comprehensive schools before being appointed as headmaster at Hollyfield. He described Hollyfield as friendly with both pupils and staff being approachable. He was very clear that the vandalism and rudeness seen at some of his previous schools was not present at this school. Unlike his predecessor, Mr Harries was against grammar school education and thought that children could not be classified into academic and less academic at 11 years of age. He also thought that the same curriculum should apply equally to girls and boys, not always the prevailing view at the time.

Mr Harries was a relatively young and energetic headmaster and as, according to pupils, he drove his mini car fast and also because he consulted both staff and pupils about new ideas he soon became a popular headmaster. Although constrained in many respects by the Local Education Authority, he was a curriculum innovator and an advocate of greater curriculum choice for pupils. The punishment book reveals Mr Harries to be a regular user of corporal punishment, mainly by one or two hits across the bottom by a short and flexible cane. However, in his Hollyvine interview he admitted to wishing that he did not have to use it but that it was necessary, even if rarely used, in Hollyfield. He was a strong supporter of the staff and would encourage innovation particularly in the curriculum. He was also a strong advocate for the school and was frequently bemoaning lack of facilities and classroom space to the Local Education Authority. This resulted in several temporary huts being added to the school buildings.

View from the top of Villiers showing Albury House, two of the huts and the entrance to Hill House. The old Kingston Power Station can be seen on the skyline. Source: Dan Leissner

During Mr Harries' time the school roll increased steadily to just over 1000 pupils with six forms in each year and a small sixth form. The first and second years had a year tutor, Miss Randall, up to her retirement in 1981, with an assistant; the third and fourth year also had

Hollyfield

a year tutor, Mrs Spink, with an assistant, and there were separate tutors for the fifth and sixth Forms, Mr Phelan and Mr Swanson. The deputy head was Mrs Serbutt and later Mr Vockings was promoted from senior master to deputy head.

Classes were mixed ability for the first year and then divided into three ability groups. French was the standard language for all with German available from the second year for the more able linguists. Options were introduced in 1979 for years four and five. The exams taken at the end of the fifth form were the General Certificate of Education Ordinary levels (O levels) and the Certificate of Secondary Education (CSE).

The uniform was maroon. There was clearly a lot of debate at the time about the uniform as maroon was limited to two suppliers who seemed to parents to charge high prices and maroon was, judging by the pupil letters in Hollyvine, not a popular colour with many of the students. In 1978 blazers cost from £12.90 and ties were 74p. School badges were bought separately from the blazer and sewn on and cost 57p. Some pupils were allowed an exeat for the lunch break and could go home!

The maroon school badge
Source: Dan Leissner

In 1978 parents were asked to contribute to the school fund at 20p per term for the eldest pupil in the family and 10p for the second and subsequent child. The parents had the Hollyfield School Association (HSA) as a social and fundraising body and family life membership was 50p. School began at 8.50am and there were eight periods a day with the first lesson being 50 minutes long to incorporate assembly on certain days and each of the remaining lessons being thirty five minutes. Lessons were often timetabled in doubles to give time for practical work and the day was split with four lessons on the morning with a twenty minute mid-morning break, and another four lessons in the afternoon with five minutes allowed to get from lesson six to seven. School ended at 3.45pm.

Joan Jecock (right) with Marian Gordon (now Pinkus) at Joan's leaving party
Source: Hollyfield archives

One person who would have known more about, not only Mr Harries but also Mr Annets and Mr Humphreys would have been the school secretary Joan Jecock. She worked in the Albury office as secretary and later as the first Bursar, from 1968 to the end of 1984. She once described with great hilarity, an event at an evening meeting for parents when Henry, the adopted school cat, came from nowhere and joined Mr Harries on the stage during his talk. Her comment in the school visitors book on 20 December 1984 upon her retirement reads "Gone – but not forgotten, I hope!"

Probably the greatest threat to the continued existence of Hollyfield came in 1984 when the under pressure Local Education Authority (LEA) proposed a re-organisation of secondary schools to cope with a projected reduction in the secondary age population of about 2000 across the age range by 1989. It was proposed that either Kingston's Tudor School, Chessington's Fleetwood School (later to be Chessington Community College) or Surbiton's Hollyfield could be closed to compensate. A meeting called jointly by the school, its Parent Teacher Association (PTA) and the Governing Body, was held in the school hall in February and was packed out with parents, teachers, pupils and friends of the school. Feelings against the LEA plan were strong and Declan Terry, then the chair of the PTA (and later to become chair of governors) stated "We will not stand idly by and watch our school be dismantled sold or disrupted." He argued that compared to the other schools Hollyfield was the most efficient having a low expenditure per pupil and also that its closure would dramatically affect the percentage of co-educational places available in the Borough, resulting in a "massive reduction in parental choice". He also vowed to "fight dirty" to protect the school if necessary. At the end of the meeting the motion that Hollyfield should continue as an 11-18, co-educational school with six forms of entry was carried unanimously.

The resistance and community solidarity generated from this meeting clearly had an impact as Hollyfield was left untouched and in 1984 Tudor School in the north of the Borough closed. This was unfortunate for that part of the Borough as Tudor school had only been created in 1980 from the existing Rivermead Boys' School together with girls displaced from the closure of Bonner Hill School. The Conservative administration, who had led this Kingston re-organisation, then moved the selective Tiffin Girls' School into the vacant building the following year amidst hoots of derision from the opposition parties. This left north Kingston without a secondary school and ironically swelled the number of pupils heading out of Kingston to Grey Court and Teddington schools in Richmond as well as increasing the Kingston population attending Hollyfield.

Throughout this time Mr Harries had to manage a very worried set of staff, pupils and parents and a whole succession of meetings was held until it was known that the result was favourable to Hollyfield. A further subsequent irony is that some years later, in 2009, the Local Authority held another consultation regarding education in the north of Kingston with the proposal that a new eight form entry school be built ready for 2013/14 to cope with a rather rapid population growth.

Working from his office directly opposite the main front door of Albury House, one of the difficulties that Mr Harries had to deal was a drunk gardener. This caused concern amongst the pupils as Tony used to shout and swear loudly. When he was eventually sacked Mr Harries could be seen pruning and cutting bushes on some days after school until a replacement was found. Staff and pupils were curious one morning when a teacher was seen sitting in his car in the car park instead of teaching his classes. He had presented Mr Harries with the information that he had been arrested for an offence of indecency and was waiting whilst Mr Harries conferred with the Local Education Authority. The teacher was never seen again.

Mr Harries was also headmaster during some of the teachers' strikes particularly those by the National Association of Schoolmasters Union. As he was a good supporter of his staff and did not want pupils to miss classes he would sometimes cover classes for these teachers who were striking for more pay by refusing to work full days and was generally sympathetic of such action.

Eileen Serbutt had been the deputy headteacher to Mr Harries since 1978. As his deputy she worked from the office on the left as one enters Albury House. In 1985, Mr Harries was seconded to the Local Education Authority (LEA) to lead Kingston's curriculum contribution to the national TVEI project (Technical and Vocational Educational Initiative). Initially this was for one year and Mrs Serbutt was appointed by the governing body as acting headteacher. A further one year extension was announced to the TVEI project and when later it became clear that it would be a permanent feature then Mr Harries' post as headteacher was fully taken over by Mrs Serbutt from September 1987.

The pastoral years 1985-1993 (Mrs Eileen Serbutt)

Eileen Serbutt was Hollyfield's first and to date, only, substantive female headteacher. Like Iowerth Harries before her, Eileen Serbutt was from Wales and her parents were teachers. She was born in Swansea and following her schooling went to Manchester University to study English. After graduating she worked for the British Medical Journal for six months before deciding to do a PGCE course at Cardiff University to become a teacher. She came to Hollyfield via Llanelli

Girls' Grammar School in South Wales, Rosa Bassett Secondary School in Tooting and Mayfield Girls' School, Putney. At Hollyfield, in addition to her deputy head and headteacher work she taught English, religious studies and general studies. In an interview for Hollyvine in 1986 she described her move from the ILEA, the well funded Inner London Education Authority, to Kingston as moving back in time due to the lack of resources and the old style formal teaching. She also described how education had changed substantially in the early eighties with different teaching methods and new pastoral systems. She was in favour of greater consultation with parents and also of the new GCSE examinations provided they were funded adequately. Mrs Serbutt was also busy out of school with her interests recorded as belonging to a choir, being a church warden and being a member of the London Appreciation Society which apparently involved local walks and outings. She was also a self-confessed bibliomaniac.

Assisted by her three deputy heads, Mr Vockings, Mr Forrest and Mr Forward and under the heavy aegis of the Local Education Authority, Hollyfield became a school where equality of opportunity was valued and the comprehensive ideal engendered. The new pastoral system initiated by Mr Harries was further developed and a Dyslexia Unit, otherwise known as the Special Skills Unit, set up in a hut newly placed in the corner of the staff car park. This unit took up to 12 pupils with dyslexia as a specific learning difficulty and they were largely integrated into the school with extra staff led by Mrs Shirley Street, supporting them. A unit, for Special Skills, later to become Special Educational Needs (SEN) under Mrs Myra Usher was also set up for another 12 pupils. These units were in addition to the existing Hearing Impaired Unit previously set up under Mr Annets. The units were well used by the Local Education Authority and arrangements were often made for pupils to transfer from other schools.

Staff and parents became increasingly aware that one of the unintended consequences of the greater pastoral philosophy was the behaviour of some of the pupils and the lowering of examination results. This, coupled to lingering unease about the future of the school reduced both the quality and quantity of pupils applying to enter the school. In 1988 only 96, out of a possible 180, pupils joined the first year. Only 30% of pupils entering the school in 1991 obtained the 5 A-C GCSE pass standard when they took their exams five years later and in 1992 the number of pupils entering the school was still well below capacity with a total roll of less than 700 being reached in September

1992 and the following two years. This had reduced from well over 1000 in 1980. A local primary school population drop was another factor in this but the previous uncertainty about closure together with the changed emphasis of the school and reports of bad pupil behaviour and underachievement meant that parents were less inclined to put Hollyfield as their first choice and so the school suffered. A further complication was that fewer girls than boys were now applying to join Hollyfield due the increasing success and popularity of the local girls' schools which gave Hollyfield more of a boy's school image therefore making it even less attractive to girls.

Many positive things also happened during the headship of Eileen Serbutt. The new TVEI courses came into the option system for the fourth years and were initially quite popular especially with the previous headmaster Mr Harries driving this initiative from the LEA. The Youth Club, run by parents and teachers, particularly Mrs Serbutt, flourished and celebrated its third anniversary in 1986 when the Minister for Sport, Richard Tracey came and switched on new floodlights for the playground. Because of Eileen Serbutt's direct hands on approach, the PTA was also very active with members like Declan Terry driving new initiatives such as car boot sales which ran monthly in the large playground on sunday mornings for several years, contributing thousands of pounds to the school.

In 1987 the school celebrated its 50th anniversary. The actual anniversary date was in the half term holiday and so the school ran a fun day for the pupils after their exams and also held a Golden Jubilee dinner. This was notable in that not only did the Mayor, Mrs Jenny Philpott attend but also the previous headmaster Olsen Humphreys although due to failing health this was to be his last ever visit to the school.

Teaching for the new GCSE courses also started in 1987 for pupils in the fourth year. This required extra training for the teachers and much effort in writing new schemes of work. GCE O levels and CSE's were phased out although many teachers and pupils were left wondering why, particularly when the GCSE's were found to have entry possible at both foundation and higher levels. Mrs Serbutt was concerned about both the cost and the appearance of the maroon blazers. They were expensive and tended to get rather tatty towards the end of the year. After consulting with parents in 1987 the maroon blazers were replaced by black blazers as is still the case. The maroon jumper remained and was eventually replaced by a black one in 1991.

*The maroon skirts and jumpers.
The teacher taking the register is Colin Mason, the Head of Maths.
The room was Villiers 8, now one of the Sharman Science laboratories.
Source: Hollyfield archives*

Finance became of greater significance to the whole school from 1989 as it became fully responsible for managing its own budget. Previously Surbiton Central School and later Hollyfield were mainly dependent on the Local Education Authority, Surrey first then Kingston upon Thames from 1965, for its resources. This meant that it was the local authority that determined teacher numbers, maintenance, buildings and grounds, contracts, departmental allowances and all other aspects of the running of the school. Under the new scheme, called Local Management of Schools (LMS), the school received a delegated budget and could manage it as it wished. Instead of having only £60,000 or so annually to spend on its resources the school was now suddenly responsible for a budget of £1,500,000. This gave Hollyfield a much greater level of financial freedom and self-determination and potentially gave it impetus for improvement. The budget was managed, in liaison with the governing body, initially by Mr Garland and then by Mr Forward.

Other events during the headship of Mrs Serbutt seemed to bring important female visitors to the school. These were seen as providing good role models for girls with the aim of attracting more to even up the gender balance. In October 1988, the new Cedars House was opened by Angela Rumbold, Minister of State for Education. The two old Horsa hut science laboratories for physics and general science were demolished and two temporary huts on the front lawn under the cedar trees used for IT and technology, removed. The temporary RE Hut, the base for Miss Rachel Dawe, was also removed from the Villiers lawn. Cedars House, named after the two large and distinctive trees on its lawn opposite Albury House, was originally designed with a toilet block attached but rising costs meant that only the eight classrooms with attached offices could be afforded. The caretaker was not too happy about the loss of part of its garden for its construction and pupils had to endure another 20 years, until 2008 when New Sharman was constructed before they had another decent set of toilets. Cedars House became the base for modern foreign languages (French and German initially and Spanish later) downstairs and history, Religious Education and Government and Politics upstairs. Although it was a nice new block, described as "a showpiece study block" by the Surrey Comet, it did not take pupils and staff long to realise that the rooms were cramped and the corridors too narrow with frequent crushes occurring at the entrance/exits at lesson changeover.

In 1992, following a significant refurbishment of its science laboratories and geography rooms, Villiers House was re-opened by the astronaut Helen Sharman and renamed Sharman House in her honour. Helen Sharman lived nearby and had already visited the school since she became the first British astronaut. The other significant female visitor was Lady Parkes who also came in 1992 to open the refurbished Hill House technology department. Gradually, it seemed that after many years, the premises were being improved and the buildings were being made more attractive to both current and potential pupils.

Other events during this period included the start of the new national curriculum in 1989. It began for Year 1 and went all the way up to GCSE over the next five years. Records of Achievement were introduced and the first award ceremony was in July 1989. The school was a pioneer for this new initiative and it required a massive administrative input to produce all the documents that were supposed to be in the burgundy coloured folder that each Year 5 pupil received at the end of the year. Information Technology (IT) was developing all the time and the new BBC computers were being used in maths and science lessons regularly.

In 1990, following the trend of the national curriculum which followed through four Key Stages covering the eleven years of education from 5-16, the pupil years in the school were renamed Years 7 – 11 with Key Stage 3 covering Years 7,8 and 9, and Key Stage Four, Years 10 and 11. Each Key Stage terminated with tests such as the infamous SATs (Standard Assessment Tasks) making this generation of pupils the most tested ever. Most teachers felt that the heavy assessment regime had the effect of stultifying the curriculum as teaching became mainly focussed towards passing the test rather than enjoying the learning of the subject.

Aerial view of the school circa 1990 showing the red tiled roof of the newly built Cedars House.
Source: Hollyfield School archives

*The Hall with GCSE examinations in progress, 1990.
From the left the teachers are Mrs Huckle (English), Mr Garland
(Maths), Mr Escott, Mr Usher and Mr Cummings (Science).
Source: Hollyfield archives*

The school received several prestigious awards over this time. In 1990, thanks largely to the work of Mr Vockings, it received the Borough Environmental Pride Award. Although only a local award this was significant as Hollyfield had prised this away from the seemingly permanent grip of the local girls' schools and it reflected the improvements that the school was working hard to make. In 1992, the school received the national Schools Curriculum Award. This was a real coup and reflected work put in by many of the senior staff of the school who were determined to see the good work that was going on across the curriculum be recognised. This was followed, in 1993, by an award of £200,000 under the national Technology Schools Initiative (TSI) following a series of detailed bids by Mr Forward and Mr Chandler. These awards, by respected third parties, were significant in that they were generating greater pride amongst the staff and pupils and causing many to view the school more positively.

Eileen Serbutt in her office 1992.
The maroon uniform for the pupils has gone.
Source: Hollyfield archives

There is no doubt that Eileen Serbutt worked tirelessly to serve the school as Headteacher, frequently putting in long hours including many evenings and weekends. She had a good sense of humour, an impressive ability to make a point effectively and was a champion of good relationships both within and outside of the school. She held strong values of right and wrong and would not hesitate to stand firm against actions by anyone not in line with her positive view of the school and its role.

Mrs Serbutt retired from the headship of Hollyfield in August 1993 after which she continued with her church work, taking up the role of warden at St Mary and St John the Divine, Church of England church in Balham, south London. She later became ordained and, in 2010, as the Reverend Eileen Serbutt, was still continuing with her life-long commitment to pastoral work as assistant priest at the same church. Mr Forward, her deputy head, was then appointed as acting headteacher for the autumn term 1993 until a new substantive headteacher was appointed and took office the following January. A significant initiative during this time between permanent headteachers, was that a new school behaviour code was introduced. Developed by staff working groups it was based on the notion of positive discipline and consisted of 10 classroom rules and 10 general rules which, according to an interview given by Mr Forward to the Surrey Comet, improved the tone of many lessons and made a significant difference to behaviour throughout the school.

Becoming an outstanding school 1994–current (Mr Stephen Chamberlain)

Stephen Chamberlain was born in Australia and then moved to England where he went to Lowestoft Grammar School in Suffolk before studying English and history at Sheffield University. He taught for 17 years in schools in Lincolnshire, Ealing and then at Stepney Green School in Tower Hamlets as deputy head and acting headteacher, before being appointed to the headship at Hollyfield. Prior to his arrival he had resolved to re-energise the school and to make it as popular and as successful as it deserved to be.

Upon his arrival in January 1994 he saw every teacher teach in his first six weeks and then restructured the Senior Leadership Team (SLT) and brought in a new line management system with a new meetings structure. He also worked on improving liaison with Primary schools and identified three key areas for pupil improvement; recruitment, attendance and achievement. He worked with staff to effect a new mission statement, a new style prospectus with colour photographs on the outside of a folder with layered information inserts. He also reinforced the new behaviour code and added an emphasis on the Home School Partnership. The number on roll was described in the

1994 prospectus as 750 with 100 in the Sixth Form. This was a low number for a school with a capacity of over 1000 which a new start, including the new headteacher and the new prospectus, was intended to improve.

Stephen Chamberlain.
Source: Hollyfield archives

The school's first inspection by the newly formed Ofsted (Office for Standards in Education) occurred in March 1995 when about 17 inspectors descended on the school and watched lessons, assemblies, meetings, clubs and the playground. They also interviewed staff and pupils and saw everything that happened for a week. Then they left having briefed Mr Chamberlain and said several positive things about the staff and pupils and about the tone and atmosphere of the school and its quality of teaching and leadership. This was then relayed to the staff at a meeting together with some of the Governors and was followed by a big party in the staff room. An additional reason for Stephen Chamberlain celebrating was that throughout the inspection he was doubly nervous not only because his leadership was under scrutiny but also because his wife was about to give birth to their second child. The school was given, as expected, an intermediate grade but the inspection team were complimentary about the new headteacher and his leadership team and Mr Chamberlain was challenged to take the school forward from "good" to "very good" and towards "outstanding" – the top Ofsted grade.

Under Local Management of Schools (LMS), the school, whilst having a delegated budget was still heavily under the control of the Local Education Authority (LEA). This prevented the school from being autonomous and self-determining as the LEA had interests in all local schools and would not allow Hollyfield to progress as it could be to the detriment of others. By careful preparation and a number of business orientated presentations in 1994 and 1995 Mr Chamberlain and Mr Forward convinced most of the staff and governing body that balloting to become a Grant Maintained (GM) School, which would delegate to it full responsibility for staffing, premises and budgets, would serve the school better. The majority of the governing body agreed and a campaign set up in parallel with an official ballot of parents began. This was not an easy decision and sadly led to the resignation of Declan Terry, who had been an excellent chair of governors and also to some vocal and orchestrated opposition from a minority of teachers and parents. However, the ballot, conducted in November 1995, was successful and Hollyfield had its GM Incorporation Day on 3 July 1996.

In September 1996, a new school day based on 6 x 50minute lessons was introduced. Intended to ensure that lessons had more "pace" as recommended by Ofsted, the day started at 8.45am and ended at 3.20pm. This further confirmed that real change was occurring at Hollyfield with a greater emphasis on behaviour and individual pupil achievement being apparent. Mr Chamberlain was always careful to obtain the authority of the Governing Body in liaison with staff before introducing change and also took time to explain things to the pupils in assemblies. Becoming Grant Maintained (GM), allowed the school to separate from the LEA and to set up all its own budgets and contracts with banks, personnel bureaux, auditors etc and to appoint more administrative and ICT staff to support the new responsibilities it now had.

From September 1997, in order to reflect the new self-determining character and image of the school, the name was subtly changed to The Hollyfield School. The following year, as if in support of the changes that had occurred, the school was visited by The Right Honorable William Hague MP, Leader of the Opposition, with quite a national and local entourage. As a further part of his re-energising programme, Mr Chamberlain also reviewed the marketing of the school and a new style glossy and more informative prospectus was produced. Another key development was the introduction of a fast-track group in year 7 for which pupils were selected via the LEA's 11+ test. This was a further very popular move and meant that even more parents, pupils and other schools were taking significant notice of The Hollyfield School as it improved in almost every respect. In 1998 the school's second Ofsted was positive about overall school improvement although critical of some aspects of the sixth form. This led to a rapid reorganisation of the sixth form team and a renewed focus on this part of the school. Due to the two largely favourable inspections, coupled to improved GCSE results with the benchmark 5 A – C up to 48% by 1998, the school, whilst not yet outstanding, was starting to improve academically and to slowly regain its popularity.

The governing body, now led by Dr Michael Morton, proved to be a great support to Mr Chamberlain and the staff as they sought further improvement. This was confirmed in October 1999 when the LEA inspectors officially confirmed Hollyfield as the most improving secondary school at GCSE in the whole Borough over the three year period 1996 – 1999. It had been a period of great change but it was clearly working and this encouraged and inspired the school, its staff and its governing body, to continue to seek further improvement. Receiving feedback from pupils, parents, governors, staff and the Local Education Authority, further new initiatives were introduced: Target setting for pupils linked to termly meetings for parents; a new music technology suite; the pioneering use of "Bromcom" electronic registration, subject of a feature article in the Times Educational Supplement; and the sixth form joined with the sixth forms from Chessington and Southborough schools to form a more efficient unit known as "The Kings Collegiate". Improvement was real and in 2001, Hollyfield received a prestigious national award from the Department for Education for being one of the most improved schools in the country at GCSE level.

There were still further improvements to be made and Mr Chamberlain pressed ahead with them. Some were physical such as the new maths block, Oak House, opened by the local MP Edward Davey in September 2002, whilst others were academic such as the use of the "Bromcom" computers to provide parents and pupils with three assessments a year and others were whole school, such as Hollyfield's new status as a Technology Specialist College from September 2003. The School Development Plan, the key document which contained all the new initiatives, seemed to get larger rather than smaller each year as every area of the school was subject to scrutiny and improvement.

Kingston MP Edward Davey opening Oak House in September 2002 Stephen Chamberlain the Headteacher is standing with the pupils.
Source: Hollyfield archives

However, threats to the school were never far away and in September 2003 the school behaviour code was tested when the Surrey Comet majored with the story of a pupil suspended for coming into school with a skinhead hair cut. The newspaper showed a picture of the boy and his Mum holding the pair of scissors which had apparently slipped and left the boy with an "embarrassing bald patch" which led her to shave his head to remove it. Mr Chamberlain held firm on the rule and on the punishment explaining that it was to prevent any gang culture appearing as it had done in other schools and to prevent possible racism and aggression which skinhead haircuts symbolise. This confirmed the new, tougher discipline stance at Hollyfield and complemented the improved academic results. All this was noticed by pupils and parents and as a consequence, by September 2003, the school roll had risen to over 1000 pupils including 100 in the Sixth Form. This was a significant milestone but it had taken nearly 20 years to overcome the consequences of the negativity generated by the threat of closure of the school by the Local Education Authority in 1984.

Probably one of the most difficult times for Stephen Chamberlain during his headship was leading the school at the time of the death of the pupil Matthew Lennon in August 2004. Matthew, aged 15, was pulled unconscious from Lake Constance whilst swimming with a school friend whilst on holiday. He was the eldest son of Clifford (Cliff) Lennon, an assistant headteacher at the school and Sally-Anne Lennon, an ex- Hollyfield pupil and previously a peripatetic music instrumental teacher at the school.

Although Matthew was flown to St George's Hospital in a coma, he died two weeks later. The verdict, given at Westminster Coroners' Court, was misadventure with the cause of the Sudden Adult Death diagnosed as heart failure. This was a great shock to the family as well as to the school community as Matthew was a very popular and fit young man who did many sports including swimming. He was also a very able student academically as well as an exceptionally talented musician who contributed to many school events and always approached life in a positive and cheerful manner. Mr Chamberlain paid tribute to Matthew by stating: "All who knew Matthew will mourn his passing with the deepest sadness. He was a fine young man, a great friend to many and an excellent student." A book of condolences was set up in Albury House and flowers, many with messages of remembrance and sympathy attached, were left under the photo of Matthew pinned to the Cedar tree on the front lawn of the school. Many pupils, staff and parents spent some time there. Grief counselling was offered to students and staff who wanted it and this continued for the first week of the new term. Matthew's funeral was held in St Mark's Church adjacent to the school and was more of a celebration of a successful life rather than an untimely death. The church was packed and many people had to stand. The Hollyfield community spirit, both managed and spontaneous, was much in evidence throughout this most difficult time.

Although some new building had taken place, such as Oak House in 2002, the growth of the school was generating high levels of wear and meant that space was tight. The insides of the buildings were relatively well maintained with a proper painting schedule and new carpets gradually replacing floor tiles but outside, buildings such as Albury house and the Horsa huts, which the school still used for music and its cafeteria, were expensive and difficult to maintain. Some improvement occurred in 2005 when the new Multi-User Games Area (MUGA) was built on the old staff car park and staff parking was relocated to the Albury lawn with an access road around the back of the school hall. Even this was not easy as some staff cars became stuck on wet days and several layers of gravel over subsequent years were required to stabilise it.

Sharman House – the extensions above the windows are sun shades. The Welsh flag in the window of the Geography department belongs to Mr Hughes.

Other work was occurring outside the school as, starting in 2005, the A240 junction at the traffic lights was realigned and whilst the school lost some land it gained a new and much improved landscaped frontage on Surbiton Hill. The new metal fences which were also constructed added greatly to the appearance and the security of the site and, with a final piece of fencing soon added along Surbiton Hill Road, meant that for the first time ever the school and its pupils were properly fenced in! A more popular addition was the construction of an impressive large white canopy over part of the playground between the music huts and Sharman House. The table benches which were installed using PTA money were immediately well used as "The Dome" became a social area for pupils particularly on hot or wet days. It

Hollyfield

also became a venue for occasional music concerts and even some lessons!

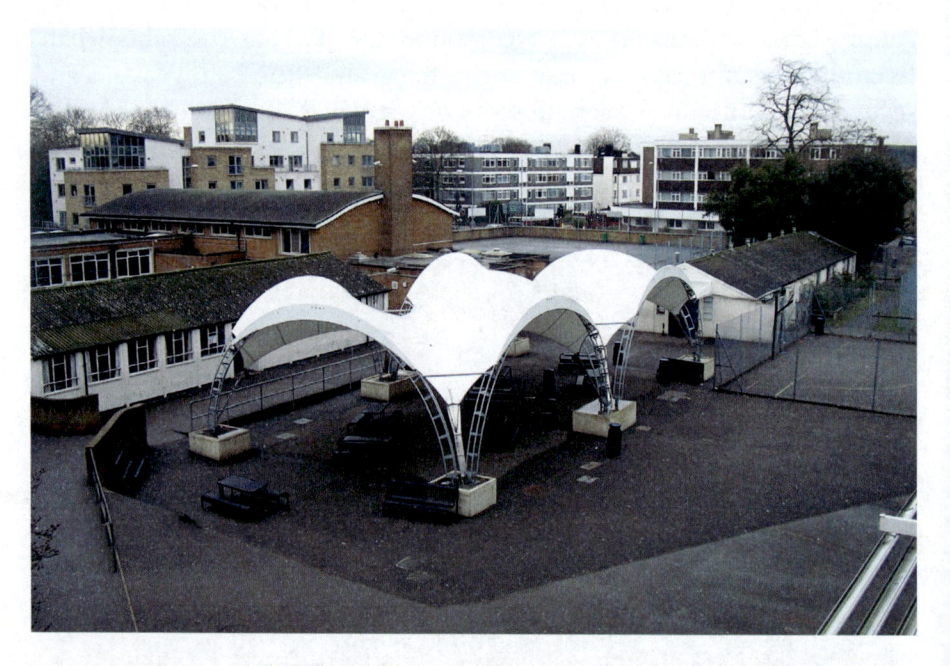

View of "The Dome" from Sharman House. The other buildings anti-clockwise from the right are the Cafeteria, playground, Gym, Food block and Music.

The following year, with over 150 now in the sixth form, work began on extending Sharman House (formerly Villiers) after first removing the English hut on the lawn. A large construction project was begun in the middle of the school site to include; on the second floor, a sixth form common room and facilities; on the first floor, three IT rooms and a conference room; and, on the ground floor a new student services reception plus a Learning Resource Centre (LRC) with 60 computers as well as book resources, offices and teaching areas. Unfortunately the original contractor went into liquidation half-way through construction and so the project was delayed whilst another was found leading to an eventual completion in September 2008. It took even longer to sort out the heating and the lack of drainage under the ground floor but the impact of the new glass fronted modern building in the centre of the site was impressive.

*New Sharman House at the top of the drive
with Cedars House to the right - 2009.*

The school continued to have a reputation for its plays which was further enhanced from 2001 onwards under the new head of drama, Marianne O'Shea, with the hall always packed out every night when a play was on. Music continued to thrive under Clifford Lennon, Tim McVittie and then Sarah Neville with large numbers of pupils doing extra music instrumental lessons in the newly refurbished music practice rooms in the Albury dungeons. The annual junior and senior music festivals were popular and St Mark's Church was always full for the annual carol service. With their new computers the music rooms, although still in the Horsa hut, became a much greater attraction to more pupils than had been the case in the past.

Sport enjoyed a massive revival started by Bill Parton but considerably extended by Dan Newman and his team of PE teachers. The house system was revived in 2008, with three new houses Osprey, Falcon and Eagle, based on two whole forms in each year allocated to each house. The aim of this was to improve belonging and competitive sport and this certainly worked as sports day, always a moderately competitive affair, was transformed with real support and great competition. Football, cricket and rugby league teams were increasingly successful as was the school's athletics and cross-country teams. The year culminated in a Mr Newman spectacular, the Sports Personality of the Year awards which always seemed to take place on the hottest evening in July, but despite the baking conditions in the school hall, was still a very popular annual event.

Oak House and The Stables - 2009.

The school's use of Information Technology was also expanding during this period. By using the additional grant income received as a Technology Specialist College the school was able to purchase over two years a laptop for every teacher and install a digital projector in every classroom. This made a large difference to the quality of lessons as well as allowing the use of data-logging and control technology in lessons, hitherto not possible. The addition of three new IT rooms in the New Sharman building together with the additional 60 computers in the LRC considerably extended the facilities and the work required from Mr Wyld and his two ICT technicians. In 2008 Hollyfield was the first secondary school in the Borough to receive the ICT Mark confirming its status as a Centre of Excellence both for the subject and for ICT use across the school.

The progress made by the school under the headship of Mr Chamberlain to date has been very significant and this is confirmed by several sources. Firstly, when Mr Chamberlain took up post in January 1994 the school had its lowest ever roll of 668 pupils comprising 442 boys and 226 girls with only about 80 students in the sixth form. By January 2009 the school's popularity had improved immensely and the school roll had grown to over 1100 including more than 200 sixth formers with the proportion of girls also improving, albeit slowly. Secondly, and a related factor, the school's 5 A* – C examination results had increased from 30% in 1996 to 80% in 2009 and the Sixth Form A level pass rate whilst holding steady at around 97% rose to a high of 669.7 average points per pupil in 2009, a year on year increase every since 2006. Thirdly, the Ofsted inspection in 2008 not only categorised the school overall as "good" (still one grade below the top grade of outstanding) but also indicated that it had a good improvement capacity and was likely to improve further in the future. Fourthly, the Surrey Comet, not always favourable to the school, wrote a special "School Report" in May 2008 which described the school as "friendly and supportive" with a 200 plus sixth form in a new sixth form centre. It referred to Hollyfield having the very favourable ratio of one computer per three pupils and to the school being the first secondary school in the Borough of Kingston to receive the ICT Charter Mark. The tide had been turned and a school once threatened with closure was now back to its previous status of being one of the best in the Borough.

This was recognised by those outside as well as inside the school, so much so, that between 2005 and 2009 over 800 applications were being received annually for the 180 places available to start in Year 7 and by 2009 the catchment area for first offers to new parents had shrunk to 1.7 kilometres from the school. This was a massive contrast from a school that could only recruit 96 pupils to its year 7 in 1988 and a real testament to the pupils, staff, headteacher, parents and governors who by virtue of their commitment, skill and determination have made the school the success it has undoubtably become. Whilst not yet officially categorised by Ofsted as "outstanding" the school is moving towards it. This current success, with the promise of much more in the future, should bring a sense of real pride to every teacher, pupil, parent and governor who has been connected with the school since its inauguration in 1937.

Hollyfield

David Forward

Pupil Memories

Les Reading (1940 -1947)

Remembers a tragic story that linked the old Hollyfield Road School with what would become its future new home on Surbiton Hill. It relates to the time when the Alexandra Recreation Ground opposite the school was used for an army and air force display. This included having a Lancaster Bomber on view. Les recalls: "The parts were transported by lorry and one day I was cycling down Surbiton Hill Road (known as 'Wagon and Horses') when a lorry carrying parts up the hill outside the Grammar School ran over and killed a school boy who fell between the cab and trailer just before I reached the spot. It was not a very pleasant sight."

Gerald Myers (1941 – 1948)

Remembers some of the early Hollyfield Road staff. He says "I clearly remember a master whose name was Mr Turner. He taught science and sports....he was nicknamed "Scummy Turner", because he often referred to offenders as "scum". He would also admonish with the phase "dirty toad". We, of the roughish boys' brigade, tried to keep clear of him. On one occasion he kept the whole class in after school in the Science room to show us an experiment. We were there for about an hour, watching him with bated breath whilst he held a rather large sealed tin over a Bunsen burner. What we were told to expect I do not recall.....but in the end all that did happen was that the tin buckled......end of experiment......time to go home!" Gerald also remembers Miss Byrne. "She taught "girly things" like knitting, and cooking and I do believe Maths, or English as multi skilled teachers were the order of the day. On one occasion she called me out in front of the class..."Myers" she said. "Yes Miss", I responded. "This paperwork is dirty, filthy," she continued. {She was referring to the pages *not* to any fact that I was writing porn} Then she added, much to my fury, "You must live in a pig sty." Do you live in a pigsty?" I must acknowledge the fact that she was not making that reference because I am Jewish but my anger was because my mother, who was a wonderful Jewish mother, kept our home spotlessly clean. Bursting with anger I turned to Miss Byrne and snapped back, "No! I most certainly *do not* live in a pigsty....You should come to my home to see it".......Cheers and clapping from the rest of the class."

Gerald was also surprised that the school taught gardening to the boys. He remembers that the gardening master, Mr Peacock, was nicknamed "Freddie" by the pupils. The garden patch was down the side of the building. There was a also a delightful Welsh master whose name Gerald cannot recall who would call pupils to order by calling out " *Boyse*, pay attention" and we would mimic him with "*Boyse, Boyse*". The naivety of the relationships between boys and girls at that time is well described by Gerald who asks: "Who of that era does not remember the bicycle shed, and taking one's "girl friend" behind it to "snog"? That was only a kiss on the cheek, or for the most forward of males a quick kiss on the lips {no tongues, we did not yet know about the use of a tongue in romance}.....That to us simple schoolboys was the epitome of love.......Kissing a girl on the lips, instead of on the cheek, was "going all the way" and something to boast about. Gerald will always remember when he told his mother that he was fond of a certain girl in the school......I said to mother " Oh yes ! she is a lovely tart".....and then, from nowhere, came her hand to my face..*Smack*..."Don't you ever let me hear you say that word again"......."Tart" to us innocent schoolboys was just short for "Sweetheart"...Nothing else....I did not find out the true meaning of the word for some time after."

Gerald also recalls one boy whose surname was Cooper. His dad had a small car business on the corner of the Ewell and Hollyfield Roads just yards away from the school. The name was Cooper Cars which was the birthplace of the Cooper Racing car who won several Grand Prix with drivers such as John Surtees, Bruce Maclaren and Jack Brabham. Several other pupils (mainly boys!) remember that sometimes they used to test drive the racing cars up Hollyfield Road by the school playgrounds with quite a noise.

Gordon Eke (1947 – 1951)

Joined the school from Tolworth Junior Boys in Douglas Road. He says that it was very daunting going from an all boys school to a mixed one with girls actually in the same class and one of the boys great pleasures was watching the senior girls playing netball in blue knickers and tight T shirts.

He also remember 1947, the year he started at Surbiton Central School being a very severe winter, as it was so cold the piles of coke used to fuel the boilers froze solid and the school closed for a week or so as the heating could not be operated. "The school buildings are very much the same as when I started, the site is surrounded by houses, a stream and two roads so there was not much scope for expansion. I guess that is why it eventually moved to the old Surbiton Grammar School site. The only additions I can recall is the building of 4 temporary classrooms in the two playgrounds. I think these were built about the time the school leaving age was raised from 14 to 15."

Regarding school dinners, Gordon says: "There was never a school canteen and dinners were served in the British Legion hall just up Hollyfield Road. I was never fortunate enough to have the pleasure of eating 'school dinners' as I lived in Beaconsfield Road, the next road to the school. From what I gathered at the time they were not quite up to Jamie Oliver standard." Gordon has fond memories of his time at Hollyfield. He says: "Academically, I was always in the top stream but not good enough to pass either the 11 plus or the 13 plus so eventually left at 15 and started a 7 year apprenticeship in the print industry in which I worked until I retired."

Some of the teachers who left a lasting impression on Gordon were a "Mr Turner (scummy), who could roll his eyes so that only the whites showed and called all pupils "scum of the earth". "Taffy Williams was our woodwork and sports teacher and we always thought he had eyes in the back of his head as he always knew who was larking about and either the blackboard rubber or a piece of wood would come flying across the room narrowly missing the culprit. He was a strict teacher but one of the most popular. Larry Lamb, our English teacher, was the exact opposite to Taffy, very quietly spoken, never raised his voice, but could control the class better than all the others and was highly respected by all his pupils. Freddy Peacock, geography and gardening, yes we were actually taught the rudiments of growing our own vegetables."

Finally, Gordon remembers that although the school did not actually celebrate the Festival of Britain in 1951, all the senior students were taken up to the South Bank and spent a day looking round the exhibition sites; The Dome of Discovery; The Festival Hall; The Skylon and The Shot Tower, where they were demonstrating bouncing radio beams off the moon, the latest technology back then.

Heather Parker (1951 – 1957)

Describes the new Headteacher, Mr. Humphreys as lovely. She says: "He would walk around the school in his long flowing black gown, and at first we were all in awe of him, but we eventually found that he would listen to us and we all admired him greatly."

She remembers the school buildings well: "The main building, with the main hall and office space at the King Charles Road end with the girls toilets just outside and the cloakrooms just inside the main door. I believe these were the girls' cloakrooms with the boys at the other end of the school with their toilets. In between of course were the classrooms. Upstairs were mainly classrooms, with the Domestic Science room at one end and the Science lab at the other. There were also two sets of classrooms built in the playgrounds. The classrooms were already built when I arrived at the school in 1951. Later on whilst I was there, two more buildings were built in similar style over in the field opposite facing the hall, and these became the Metal and Woodwork rooms. I still have a paper knife which I made in metalwork."

Julia Maslen (1953 – 1957)

Thinks she made a mistake by leaving the Hollyfield Road School in 1957 and going to college: "I left to go to Pitman's College for the last year - big mistake- Hollyfield was much better but I didn't have much say in the matter! I remember Mr Allan who shamed me into spelling - he was our form teacher and gave us spelling tests each morning. He was a good teacher and very nice. Miss Byrne took us for PT but as I wasn't sports woman of the year I wasn't that popular."

Carole Brixton (1954 – 1961)

Particularly remembers Mrs Jarvis, the Domestic Science teacher, because she was punished by her and told to clean the bins (the big ones) out. She and the two other girls being punished, stripped to their vest and knickers and put an apron on so as not to get their clothes dirty. The head teacher found them and was told by the girls that Mrs Jarvis had told them to clean the bins out. Mrs Jarvis was called for and when she found the children in their underwear she said "No no no, not like that", and was very shocked.

William Wilcox (1956 – 1958)

Was one of the pupils who spent a large amount of time at the annex at 35 Ewell Road. He transferred from Sloane School, Chelsea when he was 13 to attend the Hollyfield Junior Art School. His memories include: "… the Art Annexe in Ewell Road where we kids in JA1 & 2 (Junior Art 1 & 2) spent much of our time with Mr. Dyson and Mr. Strachan. As I remember it was next to the fire station, and the lower floor was where we did sculpture and pottery (there was an electric kiln), while upstairs was a large room with windows on three sides, where all the drawing and painting went on. The atmosphere was much freer there than in the main building, and someone brought in a small record player, which was allowed to be played during lunchtimes - it was how I first heard Elvis, Buddy Holly, etc. as my parents never allowed such sounds in our house! We could have walked back down to Hollyfield Road for school dinners, but I think most of us brought sandwiches, and had our lunch sitting around in the pottery room and chatting."

William does not remember Eric Clapton at all and it was only when he was at Kingston Art School a few years later when other students asked if he had known him, that he realized that Eric had been at Hollyfield at the same time as him. He does remember Miss Derbyshire, who taught him English Literature, as he got on quite well with her.

William says: "One episode I do remember clearly was a Christmas concert (1956), when the JA (Junior Arts group) were set the task of designing a set for tableaux to be staged behind the choir. I designed a full-stage, semi-transparent curtain which, when lit from the front, concealed the changing of the tableaux between carols, and disappeared as the lighting was raised behind it. This was scaled up from a small painting by all the art pupils working on the floor of the hall."

A Christmas concert in the school hall 1956.
Source: William Wilcox

Brenda Wren (1957-1962)

One thing that stood out for Brenda was a nice English teacher called Miss Barnett who could not control the class. She describes that some of the boys used to play her up and call her names. However the boys were to be defeated as Brenda describes that Miss "left to go on secondment to the USA for a year and when she came back the first lesson began as before, with the boys starting over again but she was having none of it and told them straight that she was having no nonsense. The year away did her good it seems as she had no problems after that."

Brenda was also a member of the elite Demonstration Dancing team with Miss Byrne the Deputy Head. She describes how Miss Byrne "did auditions outside school times and if you were selected then you were very privileged. The costumes were all hand made for you and rehearsals were hard work; any constant absentees were ousted. Miss Byrne was a stickler for accuracy to the dances whether it be a Scottish Reel or Tarantino. It was great fun and we put on a show annually to the rest of the school and parents too. It helped me to shine at something I was really good at."

Graham Wilson (1957 – 1961)

Played in the school cricket team and captained the football team. He also captained Livingston House (colour yellow), in his final year. He remembers that the football matches were played across King Charles Road in Alexandra Park. Graham was also a school prefect and should be easily remembered by others as he was the tallest pupil in the school at 6' 5". He particularly remembers Mr Humphreys as the headmaster because he confiscated Graham's chess set as he was always playing chess in class with his friends. Furthermore, he didn't get it back until he left school but he has still kept the little portable chess set to this day.

He remembers the exams being RSA and GCE (for the smart ones) at that time. He took Maths in the trailer by the far west building at the back of the school and Technical Drawing and Woodwork in the huts directly across Hollyfield Road on the Fishponds side. He also remembers having a crush on a classmate, Stephanie Carney who went on to become Mr Humphrey's assistant secretary after she graduated. He also had a crush on a Julie Comber but admits that he was too shy at the time to act on it. Graham recalls that the boys wore caps, ties and blazers and the girls, blouses and ties. Boys and girls were separated and had their own playgrounds. Not far from the school at the corner of Hollyfield Road and Ewell Road was the Cooper Racing Car garage. There was also a popular sweet shop conveniently located on the corner. Graham left the UK when he was 20 years old and now resides with his family in Canada.

Hans Gray (1957 – 1962),

Now also living in Canada, started at Hollyfield having failed the 11+ twice while at Grand Avenue. He remembers that "there were 4 streams and for some reason I was placed in 1A. This made a huge impact on me (from failure to top stream!!) It gave me more confidence." He views Olsen Humphreys, the head as an "excellent person" and also fondly recalls Mr Hann who "was my Maths teacher and later form teacher. He was the best, turned a lot of people around in Maths".

Hans says:" the only famous person I knew was Chris Dreja of the Yardbirds. I was in his art class on Wednesday afternoons at 35 Ewell Road."

Dorothy Lambert (1957-1963)

"Dot" and her husband to be were both in the same Art group at 35 Ewell Road from 1959. She thought it was great being a bit separate from the rest of the school and particularly remembers Mr Dyson the head of art who they stayed in contact with until his death. They attended his funeral along with two other ex-pupils, Graham Woodhams and Ann Murray, who also married each other.

Dot says that the third, fourth and fifth year art groups all registered together so she and her husband remember Eric Clapton even though he was in the year above them. Chris Dreja and Anthony Topham were also in the class, so Dot and her husband were among the original Yardbird groupies. Dot remembers "We only had one small cloakroom at '35' which had to be shared by all. Us girls used to pretend outrage when Eric and his cronies would be crammed in there, strumming away, and telling us in no uncertain terms to go away." Dot also says that it was the art group who set up the school's first debating society in November 1962 and also the first film society in 1963. She also remembers that 1963 was the year she went skiing with the school; "a very new venture in those days and, as I remember, a freezing one as no one had heard of ski wear in 1963!"

Brian Orys (1958 – 1962)

Was also a contemporary of Eric Clapton and Chris Dreja. Brian recalls that the art stream that they were in had most of its lessons at 35 Ewell Road so they were not seen at Hollyfield Road that often. He remembers that they did an end of year concert in the school hall and they used to be in school assemblies either in the relatively small school hall or, for a full school assembly, further down Hollyfield Road in the British Legion hall, which also served as the canteen at lunch times. Brian was fortunate enough to be in the A stream of the four streams A–D. He regarded Mr Humphreys as a progressive Headteacher although he was once caned by him. This arose from a casual conversation with a teacher in a corridor when Brian answered a question with "okay". The punishment was for "insolence to a teacher" as, in using the expression "okay", Brian had not only answered using slang but also, deemed far worse, American slang! This required him to stand by the steps outside Mr Humphrey's office before going in to receive his punishment which he says was administered very efficiently!

Rosalyn Allen (1958 – 1963)

Was not so enamoured with the school: "Miss Byrne used to take the girls in P.E. and she was very strict. As a family we were quite poor and for several terms my parents could not afford to buy me a kit which consisted of a short pleated navy blue shirt and a pale blue top. She ridiculed me in front of everyone and I had to wear navy blue knickers and a vest. The shame of it!! The knickers were obligatory as uniform underwear and, speaking of uniform, the girls had to wear maroon skirts, white blouses and a maroon and gold tie. I hated the colour as my hair was bright ginger and everything just clashed! We never had changing rooms or lockers and had to dress and undress in the main cloakroom."

Rosalyn also recall that her cookery exam was a disaster: "No one told me that you could refer to the recipe and I forgot to add raising agent to whatever I was making. Of course they did not rise and I got a telling off in front of the class and was told I was stupid."

Rosalyn continues: "I think one of the worst things that happened to me was in assembly. The leavers among us, myself included, had to go and discuss, with a careers officer what we wanted to do when we left. I had always wanted to be a nurse and to join the Navy. My dream was to do the training within the Navy and then nurse aboard ship. The careers teacher must have told the headmaster and at the next assembly he stood me on the stage and told the whole school that I was not capable of doing it. I was too stupid and too thick. I felt humiliated, belittled and very embarrassed." Hopefully times have changed and this would not happen in the modern Hollyfield.

More positively she remembers that in the sewing class they had to make their own aprons and hats to wear in the cookery class. Also Rosalyn recalls that she was never late for school. This was mainly due to the fact that they used to stand a prefect at the main door and if you were even a second late you got sent to the headmaster for detention

Mike Ferris (1958 – 1963),

Another ex-pupil living in Canada, describes George Mellon-Grant, the Chemistry teacher who also ran the boxing club, as a "great teacher". He regards events such as the 1962 end of year school play, the boxing events held in the school hall, the morning school assemblies announcing praise and punishment, new rules etc. as tremendous team-building exercises. He says "I'll never forget the insecure feeling of being in those pre-fabricated, almost temporary classrooms added to the back of the school during the October '62 Cuban missile crisis! The School Hall seems to have burnt itself into my mind, the stage, the climbing apparatus on the walls...it was central to the many school activities that made the school what it was...home to the gym, boxing, plays etc." He agrees with others that "the worst place was the lunch room....memories of such lousy meals," and also remembers that "Cooper Cars" used to test their racing cars on the street next to the school. In his opinion the school was "made great by a small band of outstanding teachers dedicated to the task."

Geoffrey Miller (1959-1964)

Recalls one of the comical things he was part of involved one of the male teachers and his pride and joy, a Heinkel Bubble Car. "My memory is very sketchy as to who the teacher was and who else was involved and indeed the final outcome for us all but the temptation was too much for us to resist. We picked up the car, lifted it over a fence and placed it behind the cycle sheds on the opposite side of the road to the main school buildings. The problem for the teacher was that the gateway to the sheds was only three feet wide and the car was wider than this." To this day Geoffrey says he does not know how the teacher got it out and would love to find out!

Geoffrey also remembers the great times they had at some playtimes. "This was because The Cooper's Garage was based on the corner of the Hollyfield and Ewell Roads and we were able to watch the mechanics testing the development of the Mini Cooper Cars in their various guises. I also believe that they developed the first Convertible Mini there to be used in the film Night Must Fall. If the information I had was correct they initially just cut the roof off a standard Mini which immediately started to twist and fall to bits when they took it out on the road. They then had to reconstruct it on a chassis for rigidity."

Audrey Whyman (1959 - 1963)

Recalls that the Deputy Head was Miss Nora Byrne, who taught biology and country dancing (girls only!). The other staff she remembers were: Mr Lamb, English; Mr Grant, history; Miss Barnett, RE; Miss Randall, shorthand and typing; Miss Derbyshire, who married whilst Audrey was her pupil and became Mrs Rudge, English; Mr Mellon-Grant, chemistry/physics and Mr Hann, whom she regarded as a superb maths teacher. Regarding the organization of the school Audrey says: "Children joining Hollyfield were "streamed" 1A, 1B, 1C and, in our year 1D, but not for each subject. Movement between streams happened on a limited scale at end of years after school exams. They were also put into "Houses": Green – Tennyson, Blue - Elgar, Yellow - Faraday and Red –Raeburn." At the end of the school year, each 'house' competed with each other in netball, football etc and there was a "winning" house with the most credits. Audrey remembers that "credits and debits" were also awarded for work and behaviour: "A monthly assembly was held on a Friday afternoon where those with most credits stood up and received a clap and those with, I think, 3 or more debits in the month were named and shamed!"

There was a 'Choice' of subjects in the 3rd year – girls did biology while the boys took chemistry and physics and the girls took shorthand and typing while the boys did technical drawing. Girls did needlework and domestic science (cookery) while boys did woodwork and metalwork with no mixing of the sexes! The school had a specialist "Art" stream from 3rd year where budding artists joined from other schools. This specialism was granted GCE courses, but Mr Humphreys once told Audrey that because the school was a Secondary Modern school he was not automatically allowed to provide other GCE courses, but he introduced the exam in other subjects anyway without having permission. Other pupils confirm that this was a very popular move and went some way towards counteracting the negative labelling many of them felt having failed the 11+ examination. "For school dinners we had to walk along Hollyfield Road to the British Legion Hall. School prefects were in charge (must have been a teacher, but all I remember was the prefects in charge.) The Playgrounds were segregated – boys in the one on Hollyfield Road and girls in the other one on the corner. There was strictly no talking on stairways and you had to progress in single file on the left hand side."

Audrey also remembers that in 1960 the school held a competition to design a new alternative summer uniform design for girls as an alternative to the maroon and white stripe. She thinks the competition was won by a girl in her class - Patricia Fleming. The new alternative design was in shades of grey and white with the design in a more or less vertical pattern.

Peter Needham (1959 – 1964)

Recognizes that "Hollyfield offered many opportunities" and thinks he was "very lucky to be taught by such a talented bunch of teachers." He describes "a very good English teacher called Donald Kedge who used to arrive at school on a Vespa scooter with an enormous windscreen. As a teacher, he was an inspiration! He encouraged us all to read and read. Not just the usual course stuff, but topical paperbacks. He even started a small library and after reading each book we were invited to discuss its particular merits or simply grade it according to how it grabbed us. We were taught interesting subjects like advertising and Mr Kedge alerted us to the style of writing being used to sell goods and services. He also brought the class to hysterics when he read Chaucer aloud to the class in his best attempt at an accent of the period. He did well because he kept us interested and I owe him a lot."

For maths, "Mr Hann kindled my love of geometry, which came in very useful many years later when I earned my living as a draughtsman. Another maths teacher was Mr Mount, who travelled to school from Coulsdon on a motorcycle combination. He tried to drum the basics of trigonometry into me, but I didn't really master the subject until my draughtsman days."

Peter also remembers his art teacher: "We were lucky enough to be taught by Miss Richbell. She was a real looker, probably only in her 20s at the time, and the entire school (well the blokes anyway) fancied her like mad. Oh! those double periods of art. Bliss!"

Peter's favourite place in the school was the new technical block, built across Hollyfield Road on the edge of Fishponds, containing the domestic science, metalwork, technical drawing and woodwork areas. "I remember carrying out what would be considered to be very dangerous activities in those days, particularly in metalwork. For instance in metalwork, we heated aluminium in a furnace until it was molten and poured the metal into sand moulds, forged red hot steel into pokers, dropped red hot copper sheet into a vat of acid to clean the metal, used lathes, shapers, drills and polishing mops. All this without eye, face and hand protection! Imagine that in these days? I will say though, whether or not we were careful or lucky (or both) I don't remember a single incident when anyone got injured."

In the gymnasium, Peter says it was a different matter. He describes Mr Logan, an "exchange teacher from Canada who introduced us to the game of softball. It was very enjoyable, and most kids welcomed it as a change from the usual football and cricket. The only downside was that if anyone started messing around, every member of the class was punished. Not detention or extra homework though, just good old-fashioned corporal punishment. He used to line the entire class up, we'd all touch our toes, and he'd move along the line giving each lad a whack on the bum with a large plimsol which he called the paddle! Ouch, I can still feel it now."

"George Mellon-Grant taught us science. George was a bit of a betting man and could often be seen popping into the local bookies at lunchtime. At the end of term, we'd often be encouraged to partake of a card game, probably with George in attendance. I have a friend who also went to Hollyfield and he tells the story of how George took his class to the Science Museum in South Kensingon. Evidently George was leading the class through the long subway from the tube station, when one of boys behind shouted to George "Is it ok if we smoke sir?" Without looking round, George replied "You already are boys".

Peter also has memories of things like foggy October bike rides to Speech Day at the long gone Coronation Hall baths in Denmark Road; looking up to prefects, but never becoming one himself; fearing Olsen Humphreys, the Headmaster and getting a caning from him for bunking off; and walking home with Ann Midworth, his "sort of girlfriend". Peter comments that it was "a great school" and feels proud that the likes of Eric Clapton, Anne Wood and Chris Dreja have also had The Hollyfield Experience. Regarding the fire in 1963 Peter says: "I'd heard a rumour that the gymnasium area had caught fire. Presumably it happened sometime in the night, because when I went to school in the morning it had been put out. I do remember the smell of course, but I don't remember much about the rebuilding. I don't think the school closed down or anything like that, so I imagine the damage wasn't too bad from a structural point of view. Looking on the good side, it probably meant we were spared the paddle for a while, while rebuilding took place."

Terry Hewett (1959 -1964)

Also remembers the fire but for a completely different reason. He says: "I remember the fire but for quite poor reasons I am afraid. I was at the time "playing truant" for over a week or so around that period and did not know that it had occurred. I was then nearly caught out as it was in the papers but I had not, of course, mentioned the fire to my parents. I did manage to talk my way out of that one - eventually."

Peter Lawson (1959 – 1965)

Remembers Mr Kedge as the teacher who wore huge grey flannel trousers. When he walked across the playground or around the corner by the huts the wind used to catch them and the boys laughed at him because they blew around like sails. Mr Kedge had the unfortunate nickname of "say it, don't spray it" amongst the pupils because of an unfortunate habit in that when he became over-enthusiastic, say over the Canterbury Tales, the pupils in the front row would have to dive for cover. Peter also remembers the mass slipperings in PE lessons. Mr Logan would rub chalk on a slipper and hit any offenders so hard that a great cloud of dust would appear. The slipper mark would be most noticeable for the rest of the day and would be obvious to any observant parent when a boy reached home. Peter also remembers that "Grandpa" Grant used to take the lower ability pupils. When the chairs were set up for parents evenings "Grandpa" always used to try to get a seat behind the stage curtains out of sight of the parents.

Peter attended the school during the "teddy boy" era which meant that whilst fashion was to be admired by the pupils it was a source of aggravation to the staff who tried to keep up standards. In this context Peter particularly remembers Mr Davies (Ron) who impressed the pupils by his trendiness as he was the first teacher to wear narrow trousers without a turn-up!

Kristina Powell (1960 – 1962)

Remembers that under Mr. Humphreys and Miss Byrne the boys did science and the girls did secretarial skills and the two never overlapped. She says "chemistry and physics were the boys subjects and typing, shorthand and office studies were for girls. I joined the school when I was fourteen having been at Holy Cross School but I was not happy there and moved to Hollyfield when we moved house. Miss Byrne was happy as the school was just starting to teach biology and I had learnt some at Holy Cross so I was quite useful to her." To become a laboratory technician Kristina had to take her GCE chemistry and physics later at night school.

Michael Hall (1963 -69)

Remembers the staff of the sixties with Olsen Humphreys as the Headmaster and including: Anne Wood (of Teletubby fame), English; Mr Lamb and Mr Kedge, English; Mrs Bradley and Miss Burridge, music; Mr Requena, maths; Mr Mellon-Grant, chemistry; Mr Rooks, physics; Mr Gealy, woodwork; Mr Fuller, metalwork; Mr Williams, technical drawing; Mr Swanson, English literature; Mr Grant, history; Mr Thorning, PE; Mr Finklestone, French, and Miss Gordon, art."

Chris Martin (1963 - 1968)

Was Head Boy in his final year and was a witness to an amusing administration of corporal punishment. He remembers "having to attend the Head, Mr Humphreys, with a culprit, as a witness to this lad being given the cane. The 'award' was for six of the best but after one telling strike on his backside the ensuing cloud of dust was so extraordinary that the normally stern faced Mr Humphreys had to send the boy away so he and I could wipe the tears of laughter away! No, he hadn't put any protection down his trousers."

Chris also remembers Olsen Humphreys having a wager with the chemistry teacher George Mellon-Grant about who would win when his previous school (private) played Hollyfield at cricket. Chris recalls: "The wager was accepted much to my horror as the captain and the due date arrived which coincided with my GCE English Language exam. I took the exam in my cricket whites, left early (lucky I got an A) and we then whopped his old school." Chris concludes that although it might sometimes have sounded like a school of horrors, in fact Hollyfield "was a very supportive and disciplined environment with superb teachers that taught me a lot of life skills that have stayed with me ever since."

Beverley Whitehorn (1964 – 1969)

Started at Hollyfield Road and then moved up with the school to the Surbiton Hill site at the start of her third year. She describes the move as smooth, certainly from a pupil point of view and welcomed the spacious grassy new site without the boy/girl separation that occurred down at Hollyfield Road.

She remember her school days fondly and says: "There were only about 500 pupils (no 6th form) at Hollyfield then and, apart from a path from Albury to Villiers (now Sharman), all the buildings were surrounded by grass. Although there wasn't a fast track exam, each year was streamed - a,b,c and d, according to their 11+ results. I lived way out of the catchment area but Hollyfield had an 'art stream' and because I excelled in this area, the school accepted me. In fact, I passed to get into Tiffin Girls' but my parents thought I was more suited to Hollyfield (and they were right). As a parent, I have often thought this was a very brave choice to make, especially as my brother was already at Tiffin Boys.' The art students used to go to a little studio near the fire station with the art teacher, Mr Dyson who I remained in touch with for several years. Miss Byrne had a keen interest in country dancing and we used to have house competitions at Surbiton Assembly Rooms. The school drama department was every bit as good as it is now and put on several operatic productions and I used to be involved with the make up. Miss Kinstrie taught Maths, Mr Grant taught history, my form teacher, Mr Clarke taught geography and Mr Kedge taught English. Mr Kedge was an inspiration, if only all teachers could be like him! He was so passionate about his subject, I used to hang on every word he said and can remember some of his lessons some 40 years later!

Mr Humphreys and Miss Byrne ran a very tight ship but we all knew where we stood with all the teachers, knowing exactly what would happen if overstepped the boundaries!"

"The current science technicians' rooms in Sharman (Villiers) were our toilets and cloakrooms and we could hang all our things in there all day long, confident that they would still be there at the end of the day. Those were also the days when doors got held open for teachers and we all treated each other with respect.

Hill House stables wasn't used when I was there and it certainly hadn't been built on. Art was in Albury or down by the fire station and technology was taught in the out buildings where music is now. The 6th form was introduced when we moved to the new site and as it was very small when I took my O Levels I left and went to college in July 1969."

Corinne Conroy (1964 -1968)

Also started at Hollyfield Road and remembers the delights of the singing lessons in the huts next to the woodwork room and watching red squirrels climbing in the nearby trees of the Fishponds park. She remembers Mrs White as her English teacher and Mrs Kingsley as her form teacher whom she describes as a good looking blonde with varicose veins and a big gold Rolls Royce. Corinne says that often the children were quite rude to Mrs Kingsley as well about her and that when she was seen to fall over in the snow one morning all the pupils had a good laugh at her expense. The school was strictly streamed by ability in those days and as Corinne was in the C stream the pupils were often naughty. Uniform, especially mini-skirts, were closely monitored by the teachers who used to check the length by making the girls kneel down and they would measure six inches from the ground. The skirt length could easily be shortened by rolling them up at the waist and lowered again for "measuring" but as soon as that was over the girls would roll them up at the waist again. The caretaker, Corinne recalls was called Geoff and he lived over the road from the school in the big house on the corner. "He was a lovely man, well to us girls anyway! Geoff would give us money to buy cigs or tights, they were 5 shillings then."

Sports were a highlight for Corinne and others: "We used to play netball in the girls playground and I can remember the men lined up along the fence watching us play. It was all very St Trinians, especially me. My mother would never buy the proper uniform for me as I was the third daughter and the baby of the family. I was a joker and rebellious into the bargain and went out on to the playing field in short skirt and stockings and suspenders for one game! I don't remember the telling off but it must have been bad as they got in touch with my Mum over it." Another time when Corinne was in trouble was with Miss Byrne, the deputy headmistress, whom she recalls was quite old and bandy legged. Miss Byrne taught dance and when Corinne and her classmate Vanessa mimicked her moves exactly so that the class was in uproar they were banned from dancing for the rest of the term

Regarding the move from Hollyfield Road up to the Surbiton Hill site Corinne says: "We did not want to move. It meant leaving our desks behind which had all our love interests carved on them. But of course the new school was very exciting, lovely grounds and basement rooms with, we thought air raid tunnels that came up in the head masters room! Nobody went there as we were too scared of the consequences." She remembers 3c: "with Susan, Vanessa, Gillian, Brenda, to name but a few. We had a wonderful time really. I left when I was 14 and started work as a typist, two days after my fifteenth birthday. The day we left, we all wrote on our shirts, and thought we would keep them for ever."

Leonard Simkins (1966 -1969)

Joined the school in the 3rd year just as the school relocated to the Surbiton Hill site in September 1966. He remembers that Mr Humphreys was the Head and he commanded respect because he had a great deal of respect and time for the school and set exacting standards in terms of behaviour and attitude. "The cane and the slipper were conspicuous by their presence then and I recall getting caned by Humphreys once with three strokes across the hand and on a second occasion with three strokes across the bum. Both the gym teacher and the geography teacher were reasonably free with the slipper too. The woodwork teacher was quite keen on regaining the attention of boys with well aimed chalk and, on the odd occasion, by throwing the chalkboard rubber. The TD teacher was simply violent and it was common for him to manhandle boys."

Referring to the situation where some teachers remained at the old school in Hollyfield Road, Leonard says: "The annexes at the bottom of the hill towards Tolworth were still used for woodwork, metal work and some art classes. The playing fields were at Chessington. Chemistry and physics lessons were held in the pre-war 'bungalows' in the main grounds of the school, and I think the three storey main building (Villiers, now Sharman) had just been completed when we arrived. Assembly and many lessons, of course, were still held in the Manor House. The stable block was still used, with the top floor reserved exclusively for prefects and 6th formers' recreation. I was invited up one afternoon when in the 5th year because I had gone to Kingston at lunchtime and bought the album 'This is Soul' and Donovan's LP 'Catch the Wind', each at 13s 11p, I think." Leonard concludes that "academically, the school was pretty good given its mixed profile and as a co-ed school there was always the distraction of the girls!"

Rosemary Kingham (left 1970)

Looks back fondly on her school days which have shaped her life. She says "Mr Humphreys was the headteacher - he knew everyone. Hollyfield was a small school by today's standards but gave a good sense of community. Mr Swanson, English literature and history, was a brilliant teacher and very inspiring. The staff group were ahead of their time as they instigated A level studies and supported people in applying for university. Mrs Bradley was the excellent music teacher and organised choirs. She entered us for competitions and we won many.

We were, I think, the first group of singers with the now Lord Webber and Tim Rice to sing at a London concert hall for Joseph and his Technicolour Dreamcoat. Fame! Regular trips were arranged for us to go to the Covent Garden Opera House and we saw many famous singers. Mr Humphrey's wife was also an opera singer. We were involved in many highly enjoyable school musicals and dramas including The Mikado organised by Mr Swanson, working many hours overtime. Mr Dyson was the art teacher who had connections with Kingston Art College. I posed in a bikini for a life class once for an art course he taught -unusual at that time. Mr Grant was a history teacher and a kind man.

The school was housed in an old very attractive building with pleasant ground. I was very ill in the first few years of my school life there so took a year again but I had very good support. I left and worked for 2 yrs and then went to train as a Baptist minister and was ordained - one of the first in the UK as a female. I later graduated as a Systemic Psychotherapist and am now a Consultant Family Psychotherapist."

Jane Venn (1967 – 1973)

Says: "When I started there the headmaster was Mr Humphreys who was very old school. He was 63 when he married the PE teacher from the local girls' school, and the choir, including myself, went by coach to a church in London somewhere and sang at the wedding. I've never forgotten, as we were brought back straight after the service having been offered nothing to eat or drink, we thought that was very mean. I went on the school cruise at the beginning of my 5th year, and I remember going to the volcano at Vesuvius and visiting Pompeii and I ate my first ever pizza. We flew to Naples, and then at the end, back from Venice. I've always wanted to repeat the experience, as I'm sure I'd be more interested in the ruins etc, and less in the boys on board!! In my first year the school 'group' made up of members of the 6th form were singing Seekers songs, Morningtown Ride etc, and we thought they were fantastic."

Ann Chamberlain (1969 – 1973)

Remembers that Mr Humphreys was the Headmaster. When she left she said she would never set foot in a school again but then contradicted that by later training and becoming a teacher herself!

She says that during her Hollyfield days things were very different from today. She remembers being very scared of Mrs Kinstrie who was formidable as was Mr. Clarke; both taught geography. She also recalls another teacher who "walloped" her on more than one occasion and also Mrs Tamblyn, who taught art and as she was young and pretty, all the boys fancied her. Ann's favourite teachers were Mr Gealy and also Mrs Taylor who taught her domestic science and sewing. Ann says that she can remember teachers having their dogs in school and smoking pipes in class. She was a bit disruptive and bored by school but it turned out that this was not without reason as she later found out she was not the "thicko" she thought but she was very dyslexic. After leaving Hollyfield she gained two degrees, a PGCE and has had a book published so she feels that the school let her down.

Ann also recalls that cross country was the absolute bane of her life. "The trip over to Chessington, followed by a run in tiny little shorts in the freezing cold was torture but we were a lot hardier in those days, never caught colds surprisingly. I used to bunk off a lot in the last couple of years, we used to meet in a cafe near the station which was next door to a bookies shop and we used to watch teachers popping in. I also remember speech day at the assembly rooms the year all of the boys got the cane, so unfair, but actually it didn't really do them any real harm." Ann remembers getting the slipper. Firstly she was sent to Mr Humphreys, the headmaster, for saying to a new teacher trying to establish control, "That's my name what's yours?" The Head said "If you were a boy I'd cane you" and then "he sent me to Miss Byrne, the little bow legged woman who was deputy head and she slippered me." Another incident which would not happen today concerned Ann's best friend Susan Bell who was black. "I can remember one teacher suggesting that it would be better not to associate with a brown girl! Sue and I are still friends and she still gets quite rankled about that."

Dan Leissner (1969 – 1973)

Dan reckons he only got into Hollyfield by way of a lucky twist of fate. His father wanted him to move from his existing secondary school and Hollyfield was the obvious choice as not only was it a better school but his father was also keen for him to go to a mixed school. Because space was available he was able to go straight into Form 3A. Dan remembers that in those days the streaming at Hollyfield went down to D and if you were in C or below you were regarded as pretty much a no-hoper.

He studied for CSE maths and says the CSE was viewed by many pupils and parents as a second rate qualification which you did for subjects you were bad at. He also took GCE "O" Levels and GCE "A" Levels. There was also an "S" Level – for "Special" – for those who were really good at something and Dan was invited to do "S" Level English, but failed it. Dan remembers that there were no modular exams in those days. His exam papers consisted of full-length essay questions with no multiple-choice and no course-work, just the daunting prospect of a blank answer book in which you had to do, say, four essay answers out of a choice of ten. This was very stressful and Dan recalls that in one of his "O" Level "Mocks", he was in such a state of nerves that he answered all ten questions in the time allowed, instead of only choosing four. He felt that he deserved an A grade for that achievement, but instead they failed him. Fortunately, he says, it was only a "Mock"!

Dan remembers the uniform with a blazer that was maroon until you reached the fourth year, when it changed to black, with a badge that had altered little since the 1940s. The girls always wore skirts, never trousers. They, like the boys, were all in maroon, jumpers and skirts; and skirts worn with school uniform were longer in those days. In the Lower and Upper Sixth you were allowed to wear your own clothes, within reason. Long hair was an issue but not for the sixth form who were also allowed to smoke in their form rooms, the upper stables for the L6 and "The Morgue" at the back of the Hall for the U6. The U6 also had a record player which was very popular. Also, he remembers that some of the Sixth Form drank in the Rising Sun at lunch time, whilst some of the teachers drank in the other bar!

Other Historical Links to Hollyfield

The History of Albury House

Albury House was built in 1856 during the early part of Surbiton's Victorian growth as a fine country mansion in the field bordered by the Surbiton Hill Road and Villiers' Path. Constructed by a local resident, Mr Dunnage, as his family home, the front aspect is particularly distinctive with its upright columns and the stables can still be seen as part of Hill House. It is still easy to imagine horse-drawn victorian carriages coming up the sweep of the drive past the cedar trees, depositing passengers at the front steps of the house and then progressing up to the stable yard to be met by the stable staff. Although many more modern buildings have been added to the site, particularly since 1965, the original gardens and mature trees including oak, holm oak, yew and cedar remain and add considerably to the pleasant character of the school.

At the time of building, Kingston and Surbiton were separate towns and the track up Surbiton Hill would have been muddy and precarious in winter. Villiers Path, cutting the corner from Lambert's Road to over halfway down Surbiton Hill, possibly provided a safer pedestrian alternative to most of the hill and records show that it was lit from 1869.

Mr Dunnage was a builder and used his own men to build Albury with the foundation stone still visible on the Albury wall opposite what is now Oak House, reading "This stone was laid by Helen Elizabeth Dunnage, Wife of W. Dunnage 1856".

The 1856 foundation stone of Albury House.

Censuses reveal that William and Helen Dunnage had eight children, two governesses, a cook, three housemaids, a kitchen maid and an indoor servant all living in the main house. There were also a coachman and his wife living in the coach house, presumably the rooms adjacent to the Stables, now a textiles room and the gardener and his wife lived in the lodge, which is currently the caretaker's house. William was a substantial member of Surbiton society, being the assistant superintendent of the Fire Brigade and one of the Commissioners for the Improvement of Surbiton. He lived in Albury House until he died in 1869 aged 66. Helen lived a further 27 years until 1896 with two of her sons, Arthur who was a doctor and Herbert, dying before her and another son Frank dying a year later. In 1898, the four remaining members of the family, William, George, Mary and Laura sold Albury House and moved locally to Avenue Elmers. All the family, except the daughter Helen and the son George, are buried together in Kingston Cemetery.

From 1898, the new owner was the Reverend John Francis Jemmet, but he may never have lived in the house as he was also resident in Guildford so it may have remained empty until 1902 when a Dr Williams moved in. He was best known as the producer of "Pink Pills for Pale People" In 1905 Dr Williams was joined by a Mr Waller but only for a year. In 1914 he was living with a Mr Hawkes and a Mr Wood but by 1918, only Mr Hawkes remained and by 1921 a Mr Thomas Thompson was living in the house and Henry Hawkes was living in the lodge. From 1913 to sometime after 1928, Albury was spelt as Allbury.

During 1924 and 1925 the building stood empty, whilst plans and alterations were made to change the house into a new Grammar School for boys. This project was instigated in October 1920 when a meeting was held to discuss the provision of local secondary education as no state funded secondary school existed in Surbiton although Surbiton High School did take some pupils from elementary schools on a scholarship. The principle of a boys Grammar School in Surbiton was agreed and Mr Willcocks, chairman of the Board of Governors, purchased Albury House for the new school. It opened as Surbiton County Grammar School on 16 September 1925 with the "disadvantages of a converted dwelling house, but with the compensation of delightful surroundings."

The early history of the new school is well documented in Bert Forward's 1946 booklet "Surbiton County Grammar School; The first Twenty-one Years" which informs us "The outside of the school was much the same then as now, except that in place of our present hall there was a large leaky conservatory which for 10 years to come, was to do duty as an assembly hall, dining room, art room and gymnasium. Forward also describes "The playground, or kitchen garden as it was then, presented a very different appearance from its present state, bare, part asphalt, part earth, littered with the wreckage of one time air raid shelters. In 1925 a huge greenhouse stood against the south wall; four paths converged on a pool in the centre and here goldfish still swam while the many trees were well laden with ripe fruit, a matter which soon received adequate attention." A picture held in the Kingston archive shows the front of Allbury House in 1927, two years after the new school opened, with a large conservatory attached to the Surbiton Hill end of the house where the Hall is now, partly visible behind a large hedge and a small conifer tree on the adjacent lawn. There is no visible indication in the photograph that it is now a school rather than a country house.

A photograph in Statham's "Surbiton Past" in 1931of the scenic front of "Surbiton County School" school shows Albury House looking very similar to its current day appearance apart from the minor differences of what appears to be a gravel path, no clear lawn edging, climbing plants over the house frontage and a weather station on the lawn opposite the

Albury steps. In 1935, the large conservatory, described as icy cold in winter, a hot house in summer and leaky when wet, was demolished, described by Bert Forward as occurring one midday with "a great crash of glass and to the cheers of the assembled school". A new dining hall/hall/gymnasium, currently the school Hall, and other rooms currently the A1 Drama room and associated small rooms at the back of the Hall, were then built as an extension to Albury to provide more facilities. A photograph in the 1947 edition of the Surbiton Guide shows the new Hall with trellises against the wall and plants starting to grow up them and a tall flagpole on the lawn by the Hall. Bert Forward describes the gardens as well cultivated especially during the war when he estimated they occupied about one and a half acres in total.

The use of Albury House as a school, whilst in nice surroundings, was as today, not particularly practical. Forward is unusually strong in his criticism: "If we are to be quite frank we must say that our main building has never been satisfactory as a school; it is very much a makeshift affair. Noisy and dirty; wine cellars, where every sound re-echoes, do not make ideal cloakrooms; the science laboratories, especially that for physics, are entirely inadequate; the staff room, two maids bedrooms converted into one, is dark, dismal, and hopelessly untidy." Further reference is also made to problems with the new Hall which appeared to be built on unsound foundations as cracks appeared in the walls, drainpipes bent and new doors soon became impossible to open or close. This came to a head when a large lump of plaster fell down during one of the services held in the hall by the congregation of St Mark's Church after their building was damaged by a World War 2 bomb blast. Movement of the hall is still a potential problem today and the wooden floor currently shows a substantially wider gap where the last repair was done.

The County Grammar School remained as a substantial feature of Surbiton Education until 1960 when the announcement was made that it was moving to a new site at Manor Farm, Thames Ditton. This was reported by the Surrey Comet to be nearer to the bulk of its catchment. Hollyfield moved up from Hollyfield Road and took occupation of the Surbiton Hill site in September 1966.

The house still provides some glimpses of its grand past. The passage between the current A2 and the foyer area was originally part of the old school office (currently used by the Personnel and the Finance Departments) as can be seen from the plaster decoration on the old office ceiling and by the archway by the Deputy Head's Office where there is a hole where the door lock originally fitted. Original plaster covings in the current Headteacher's office and the oak door with copper top piece in the Deputy head's office are indicators that the house has history. The coving above this door as seen from the Hall side is very ornate and a reminder of the grandeur of the house before it became a school.

Ornate coving above door in Albury House

Other features which are still visible include several original fireplaces particularly in the upstairs Albury classrooms and offices and the grand staircase in the centre of the building with its balustrade and stained glass window. The stone steps of this staircase were well worn, particularly on the lower steps and have now been covered and made safer. Similar treatment has been given to the worn servants' stairs down to the slate floored pantries (now known as the dungeons and containing two music practice rooms and several storage rooms) although the original stone back stairs can still be seen as they rise to the back of the cupboard in the current examination office. The "dungeons", now the Music practice and lessons rooms plus the drama and school records store, were at one time a refrigerated larder for storing food.

Oak door in Deputy Head's office in Albury House

In addition to the grand entrance with its columns the stained glass beside the front door of Albury also reminds us of its grand past with the Welsh inscription "Cadarn ar Cyfrwys", meaning "Strong and Subtle". This would appear to be a motto of the Williams family who lived in the house from 1902.

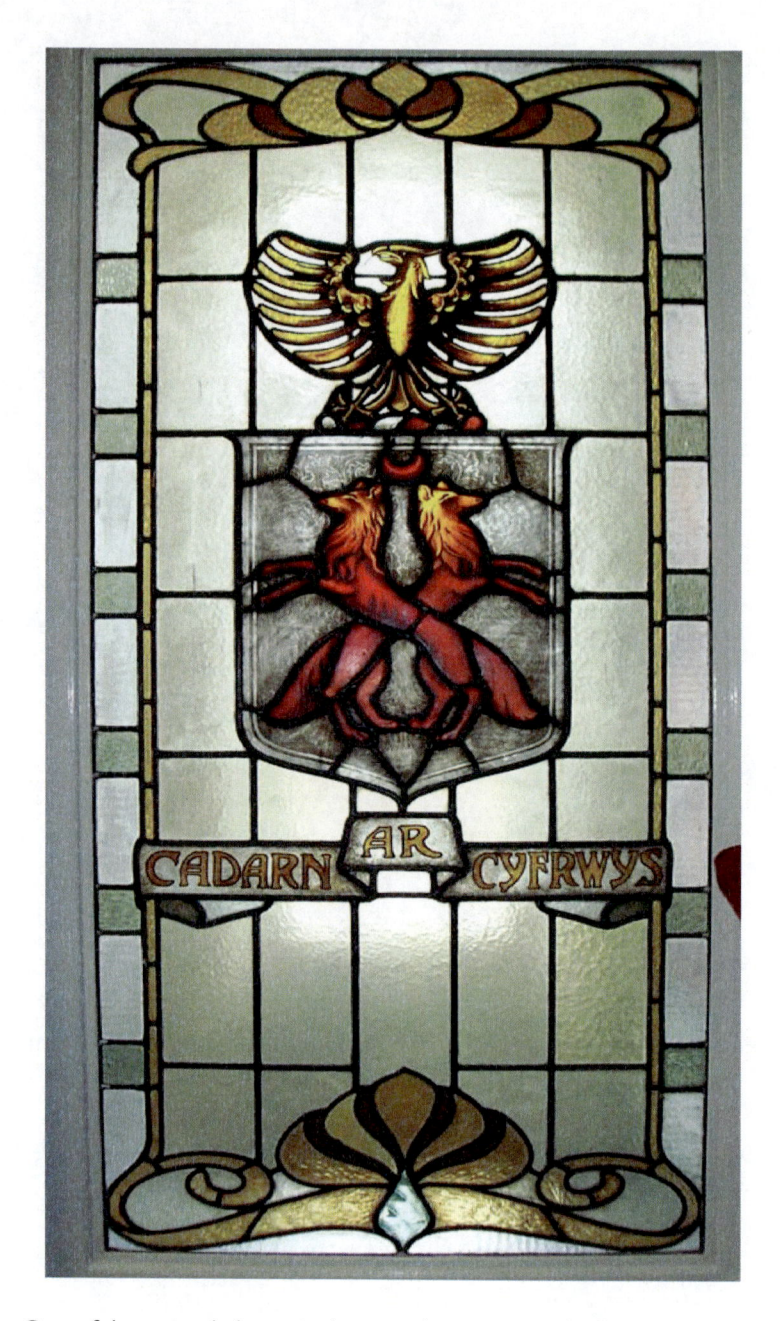

One of the stained glass windows in the entrance of Albury House

Unfortunately the grandeur of the house and indeed of the rest of the school site has not always been adequately maintained. In 1979, Albury House was described by Mr Harries in the school prospectus as "seriously in need of redecoration as are some other parts of the school". Was this really a selling point to new parents or a nudge to the local authority who managed school places? The HSA (Hollyfield School Association) reported on a decorating working party of parents that redecorated the entrance to Albury House. Either way, by the 1981 prospectus Albury House is described as recently decorated. Also for several years under the watchful eye of Mr Vockings, pupils who did not go out on trips did painting tasks during Activities Days and some of these were in Albury.

Since the arrival of Mr Chamberlain as Headteacher in 1994, Albury house has been kept in a much better state of repair both outside and inside whilst its basic character remains unchanged and it is instantly recognisable to anyone who has ever known it. The cream walls with green pillars and features show off the building well. Inside, a new Headteacher's office has been created from the old adult education rooms and a new reception and administration areas created from what was the Headteacher's office. The inner stain glass windowed doors proved too vulnerable for an increasingly busy school and were removed to the "dungeons" but the stained glass side pieces with the "Cadarn ar Cyfrwys" inscription remains. The corridors were all carpeted for noise reduction and the main stairs which were getting very worn, were also repaired and given a modern tread. Two rooms in the dungeons were converted into modern Music practice rooms with the other rooms still used for storage. The grass lawn at the back of Albury was, in stages, converted to a muddy temporary car parking area for staff and then to a more permanent stone based car park. This required a small road to be built around the side of the Hall to allow access.

The back of Albury House and the new car park 2009.

The stables – the tall entrances for the horses and the hayloft entrance are still clearly visible 2009.

The stables block adjacent to Albury has also seen a resurgence of use and has been smartened up whilst still keeping its character. The hayloft outside door can still be seen at high level although the inside of the loft is now a caretaker's work room.

The rooms where the coachman and possibly his family lived are now a textiles room downstairs and caretakers' rooms upstairs. Poignantly, in that it reflects the change of use over the years very starkly, the posts which once held the stalls of the horses are still there, albeit now in the centre of an IT room.

The "Building Schools for the Future" or any subsequent building programme is not likely to impact very much on the structure of an Albury House which remarkably, is still the main architectural feature of the school and features annually on the front cover of the prospectus.

Albury House in 2009

Hollyfield

Surbiton County Grammar School

Surbiton County Grammar School occupied the Surbiton Hill Road site for the 40 years between 1925 and 1965. Its history is therefore of relevance to the history of Hollyfield and to the history of Albury House so a summary is given here. In the early 1920s, Surrey County Council decided it was time for Surbiton to have a boys secondary school. Albury House on Surbiton Hill was for sale and was purchased on the council's behalf by WM Willcocks, the first Chairman of governors for the new school. Surbiton Grammar School for Boys opened on Surbiton Hill as Surbiton County Grammar School on 16 September 1925. It began with 69 boys and four assistant masters and soon reached a capacity of 200 with pupils divided into four houses: Villiers, Egmont, Coutts and Lovelace. The early history is well documented in Bert Forward's 1946 booklet "Surbiton County Grammar School; The first Twenty-one Years". He gives an insight into the choice of house names which in turn provides an interesting insight into the ethos that the school was trying to project: Villiers; from the Lord Francis of that name who lost his life in a skirmish with Roundheads in what is now Villiers Path at the back of the school; Lovelace and Egmont; from aristocratic 18th century owners of land in the district; and Coutts; the bankers, who did much in the 19th century, towards the development of Surbiton.

Surbiton County School circa 1927. The old conservatory stands where the Hall is now. Source: Kingston Museum and Heritage Service

In 1928, the Surbiton Guide promoted the school well: "An excellent and very up-to-date Secondary School has recently been opened at Allbury House, Surbiton Hill, under the joint auspices of the Surrey Education Committee and the Surbiton Urban District Council and known as the Surbiton County School. The aim of the school is to provide a sound general education for boys from 10 to 18 years of age. The fees are extremely moderate." The school also had the use of the playing field at Hook as the 1930 school fete raised money for the purchase and equipping of the pavilion there. The field was then described as being in a poor state having formerly been arable land and having never been sown for sports although the rough state was said by Bert Forward to confer a distinct match advantage to the home team! This is the same playing field as used by Hollyfield today which although somewhat boggy in winter due to its clay soil is quite attractive in summer and well used throughout the year.

During the war the school site was untouched despite being in a relatively vulnerable location on the top of Surbiton Hill. Nearby St Mark's Church was severely blast damaged by a bomb which landed in the adjacent St Mark's Hill Road but the school was more fortunate. Shelters were constructed and, during the particularly heavy bombing period in 1944, many school exams were taken in them. The opening to one of them is still visible by the large Holm Oak tree on the south west corner of the site and another permanently sealed entrance is in the dungeons under Albury House.

Bert Forward's history of the first twenty one years of the school is invaluable to anyone interested in the history of the school or the site. Written in 1946, just after the war, the booklet, though lacking in rigour such as dates and detail, demonstrates to those with an interest in Hollyfield that there is a strong educational history on the site. His booklet was indeed a major stimulus to the writing of this history of Hollyfield particularly because of the extraordinary coincidence of surnames and topic both of which were unknown to me prior to starting my research. Bert Forward was obviously a popular Deputy Head as one of his wartime pupils, Godfrey Smith, who became "Atticus" of the Sunday Times later described in The Surbitonian magazine Bert's "marvellous knack of making history live; Disraeli and Gladstone, previously symbols in a textbook, became real, human and fallible as he delineated them in that gentle west-country accent."

End of the day view from the front of Albury.
Note the single storey predecessors of Villiers (Sharman)
Source: David Littleproud

Boys enjoying the bank and the back lawn of Albury.
Source: David Littleproud

After the war the school was still bemoaning its poor physical state. It required additions such as science laboratories, a gymnasium, woodwork rooms and a proper dining hall plus clean and up to date classrooms. It did have a solid building in Albury House with good lawns and recreational space as well as two additional buildings, Aysgarth and Braemar, two old and rather dilapidated large houses nearer to Lamberts Road. However, it was to be another ten years before the school moved to Thames Ditton, to its new site, thereby paving the way for a Hollyfield, which had outgrown its Hollyfield Road site, to move in along with a promise of new buildings.

A description of the school in 1955 refers to only three main buildings, Aysgarth, Braemar and "School", presumably Albury. The stables and the coachman's quarters were used as the sixth form block. Braemar, one of the two large houses at the north end of the site facing onto Lamberts Road, was used as the junior school but was in a poor condition being referred to by Bert Forward as "dirty, dilapidated and infected with dry rot". He also described the rooms as so small and overcrowded that some of the boys could not face the front and he wrote that he felt particularly sorry for IIIC who were in the attic at the top of the building as it was baking hot in the summer and very cold in the winter.

Braemar just before its demolition in 1960. The photo is taken from where the Cafeteria is now. The Gym and Food block are now in its place
Source : David Littleproud

The demolition of Braemar circa 1960.
The Music Hut roof can be seen in the foreground.
Source: David Littleproud

Villiers just before its opening in 1964.
Hollyfield took over this site two years later.
Source: David Littleproud

Both Aysgarth and Braemar were demolished around 1960 although the last part of Braemar was apparently burnt down. Braemar was replaced by the current gym and Food Technology block and the new Science block known as Villiers (now Sharman) was constructed once both buildings were clear. The Science block opened in September 1964. Much of the more recent history of the Surbiton County Boy's Grammar School was documented in the school magazine "The Surbitonian" at the time but also lives on amongst members of "The Braemar Club" which was born out of old boys of the school. The Braemar Club use the Old Surbitonians Memorial Ground in Cobham, bought in 1949, and which is now known as the Cobham Sports Association.

Headmasters included AGF Willis (1945 -1950) and AJ Doig (1956 – 1964) who left just before the time that the school moved, under the headship of E Waller, from Surbiton Hill to Thames Ditton. As Mr Waller was new to the school the move was largely managed by Mr Hillyer, the deputy head who apparently used the sixth form to do a lot of the sorting and packing. The move occurred in the Autumn Term 1965 and left the site available for Hollyfield School to take it over. Surbiton Boys' Grammar School continued until about 1973 when it briefly became Esher Grammar School before Surrey County Council dropped the 11+ examination. It was then caught up in the subsequent comprehensive and sixth form restructuring and, in 1977, became Esher College, a co-educational sixth form college. Ironically, since then, Esher College has been one of the main competitors of Hollyfield in attracting sixth form students.

Hollyfield and St Mark's Church

The current school hall was the meeting place for St Mark's Church for most of the 1940s. The reason for this is best described in the words of the then Vicar of St Mark's the reverend JP Halet in the St Mark's magazine of November 1940 when he wrote that the church suffered from the effects of a bomb dropped very near the church at 4.42am on 2 October."A dignified and, indeed, noble ruin stands on a thickly populated hill, yet not one single life was claimed by the half-dozen bombs that fell on it. The building is gone; but St Mark's lives on."

As Albury House shared the same hill, Surbiton County Boys' Grammar School, who were there at that time, were fortunate not to have suffered damage. If they had, the course of Hollyfield history might also have been different. The Reverend Halet was a Governor at Surbiton County Grammar School and expressed his gratitude in the St Mark's Church magazine for the "warm and immediate welcome given to us at the County School, wherein the Headmaster and my fellow-Governors have told me that we are welcome for as long as may be."

This welcome lasted from Sunday 6 October, 1940 for a further eight and a half years. During this lengthy time the school hall was used for church meetings including for Harvest Festivals and other events. This ended when a temporary church hall was built and dedicated on 21 May 1949 in what is now the church car park. The church remained a ruin for many more years and was nicknamed "Surbiton Abbey" which from pictures is appropriate as the main building was a shell but amazingly the spire remained standing. As far as the contents were concerned, only items in the safe such as the communion plate and the parish registers were recovered intact. A restoration fund was quickly established after the bombing and grew steadily but due to pressure on resources after the war and subsequent indecision about the necessity of a church at that location it was not until the 1960s that the building was repaired. Today the repair lines can still be seen from the pavement of St Mark's Hill.

Since moving to Surbiton Hill in 1966, Hollyfield School continued to use local churches for its annual carol service. The majority of the time (excluding 1992 and 2010 due to building works at St Mark's when nearby St Andrew's Church was used), that has been St Mark's church due to its close location, appropriate size, facilities and welcome. An interesting outcome, given the historical linkages between Hollyfield and St Mark's Church, is that from the upper floor of the Sharman extension completed in 2006, there is now a clear view of the church building and spire.

David Forward

A Chronology of Events
1937 – 2009

This list and information of events is taken from the variety of sources held at the school in its archives. A key document is the hand-written school log started in 1937 and kept in various degrees of detail up to 1965.

24 May 1937 Hollyfield opens as a new school called Surbiton Central School located in Hollyfield Road, Surbiton; Headmaster Lt Col. FWC Hill OBE TD; 352 pupils on roll.

March 1939 The school is inspected and described as having made an "admirable start".

August 1939 Due to the war the Headmaster is called up to command the 67th Anti-Tank regiment. Mr FW Beale is appointed as temporary Headmaster.

September 1939 The school remained closed as trenches had not been dug. A partial re-opening took place in October with a shift system operating but it took until December for all six trenches to be dug and for all pupils to return to full timetable from 1 January. Some of the boys dug up the lawn in readiness for the planting of potatoes to assist with food shortages.

1940 Many pupil and teacher absences due to illness or war related activities including medicals and being called up. On 27 August only 67 pupils attended school at 9.00am because of a prolonged air raid warning the previous night. A few more came in later.

Hollyfield

1941 In January the school air raid shelters flooded and so pupils had to shelter in the corridors instead.

1942 Mr Hill returns as Headmaster for the Autumn term before getting recalled to the army from January 1943 to command the 96th Anti-tank Regiment Royal Artillery. Mr Cleland is appointed as temporary Head Teacher.

1943 The school was closed for a day on 5 Feb and 250 teachers trained on its site in English and Arithmetic – the first time the building was used a Teachers' Centre – a precursor of its current function.

1944 Mr Cleland the temporary headmaster was injured in a bombing raid and Miss Guyer took over as acting head for about a term whilst he recovered. Due to the severity of the bombing raids only 9 children registered on 10 July 1944.

1944 The Butler Education Act brought in the new tri-partite system of secondary education with Modern, Technical and Grammar Schools. Surbiton Central School was non-selective and so was a Secondary Modern School with the brightest children going to the Grammar Schools at 11 and 13 years of age.

1945 As the war ends, Mr Hill returns as Headmaster after serving as an officer in the army since 1943.

1946 Free milk was introduced for all pupils. This generally consisted of one third of a pint at morning break time and was intended to combat post-war under-nourishment and to provide additional vitamins.

1947 The school leaving age is raised from 14 to 15 years old.

1947 The school is referred to as Hollyfield Road Central School (rather than Surbiton Central School) in the Surbiton Guide.

1949 The school log records that there were 477 pupils on roll in January.

1949 School trips continued and included visits by various groups of pupils to the sewage works, sensibly in the month of January, to St Matthews's Church in February to hear a talk by the Reverend Chamberlain on the church and parish, and to Croydon Airport in March. In April the senior girls entered an International Dance Competition as part of the Wimbledon Festival and came third.

In October a new first appointment teacher started with what many teachers would regard as a very appropriate name: Mr Bravery! He was a temporary teacher who taught metalwork, technical drawing and some geography.

1950 The school log records a large number of visits to places such as the Library, County Hall, music concerts and competitions and, a rather notable one given modern attitudes, Carrera's cigarette factory. These, and several other work place visits, were arranged by the Youth Employment Officer.

1950 March. The school was struggling with its size and two shifts, a girls' shift and a boys' shift were introduced into the canteen to reduce overcrowding.

1950 April. Miss Byrne, a PE and dance teacher, replaced Miss Guyer as deputy head. Miss Guyer had taught for 40 years and was the original deputy head from the opening of the school in May 1937. She was presented with a set of mahogany coffee tables and a hand-cut glass vase with a silver base in assembly on her last day.
The school always had a large number of visitors, mainly from the Council but some were more directly for educational purposes. An example was in May 1950 when under the Empire Lecturers Scheme a Mrs Offenburg from Australia gave a talk on Australia illustrated with lantern slides to pupils in the 2nd and 3rd Year forms.

1950 September. The school continues to grow as in September the roll was 537 caused by 77 leavers last term and 156 new entrants. This increase was partly due to 24 Junior Art pupils who transferred from Kingston School of Art and occupied the newly refurbished upper floor Art studio at 35, Ewell Road. Amongst the new staff was a Mrs Jarvis, domestic science teacher, rather a coincidence as another Mrs Jarvis taught Home Economics (renamed Food Technology), at Hollyfield from 1997 onwards.

1951 May. Many visits took place including one to the Kingston Tannery Works on 25 May. Patriotism was promoted with St George's Day celebrated by a pageant play written by Miss Derbyshire and on 3 May the entire upper school listened to the radio broadcast of the King's opening of the Festival of Britain. The Festival of Britain opened at Waterloo on the South Bank with its Exhibition Dome and Skylon Tower and gave science and technology a much needed lift after the war. Gordon Eke (1947 –

1951) remembers that all the senior pupils spent a day up at the South Bank and no doubt many other pupils and their parents were some of the 10,000,000 visitors who attended the exhibition. On the 24 May, Empire Day was celebrated with a special morning assembly and later in the morning, a film on India with a visiting speaker with the Mayor of Surbiton, Alderman Roberts also in attendance. Pupils were also allowed home early in the afternoon.

Boxing and also Dance, led by Miss Byrne, were very popular activities at this time with several bouts and shows being put on with a high standard of attainment.

1951 A sad entry in the school log records that one of the teachers, Mr FC Peacock, who had been in post teaching geography since the school started, died following a stomach operation in Kingston hospital. He was a very popular teacher and "Freddie" was particularly remembered by pupils for his gardening lessons.

1951 September. The school roll was 563. GCE O level courses start to replace the School Certificate (SC) and the Higher School Certificate (HSC).

1952 A note in the school log by Headmaster Hill on 4 February, timed at 11.00am, records the death of King George V. "What a shock the news brought to the whole school! It has been very difficult to realise that the news is really true." The funeral was watched 11 days later on television (first ever reference) by the pupils.

1952 February. The school magazine was printed. As this is the first reference to a magazine in the school log, it is probable that it was the inaugural version and a copy is held in The Hollyfield School archives.

1952 April. The first reference to the committee of the Parent-Teacher Association in the school log.

1952 September. The school roll of 562 meant that more classroom space was required but it was another two years before the two practical rooms were constructed on the Fishponds site across Hollyfield Road.

1952 The PTA Christmas Bazaar, attended by the Mayor and Mayoress, raised £100 4s 8d which was put towards a sound projector for the school.

1953 On 2 June, two teachers, Mr Morman and Miss Derbyshire took a selected group of pupils to see the coronation procession of Princess Elizabeth to Westminster Abbey. They were part of a selected group of 30,000 pupils from different schools from all over the country given viewing places on the Victoria Embankment.

1953 July. The first school swimming gala took place at Surbiton Lagoon. Also, the first trip abroad to Belgium took place for a week in the early part of the summer holiday. This was for 26 pupils supervised by the Headmaster, Mr Hill, plus Mr Hodge and Miss Storey. They visited Holland and some of the French battlefields. This was probably a poignant visit for Mr Hill due to his wartime experiences with the Anti-Tank regiment.

1953 September. The school roll reached a record of 571 pupils.

1953 December. The PTA bazaar raised £66-9s-10d part of which went towards an electric gramophone for the music department. The gramophone was purchased but unfortunately was stolen during a break-in during the following February.

1954 July. A school trip went to Belgium , Luxembourg, France and Germany.

1954 A strip of land opposite the school on the "Fishponds" site was rented and two new temporary classrooms, one for woodwork and the other for metalwork were constructed. The existing metalwork room at 35, Ewell Road was then given over to Art and the previous woodwork room was refurbished to make a second science laboratory.

1954 December. The Christmas Bazaar raised £53-3shillings towards new maroon velour curtains for the Hall stage.

1955 April. A school trip for 53 second years went to Eire. This was followed by two further long distance trips the same year; Yorkshire for 54 pupils in May, and a fourth and fifth year Art trip to Germany in July.

1955 June. The first reference in the school log to the new GCE examinations, which began with English language followed by geography. The results for the few pupils who took them must have been good because subsequently the Governors granted an occasional day holiday on 6 December to recognise the academic and examination successes in 1955.

1955 December. Despite being a relatively poor school the school log records donations being given to others from pupil fund raising activities. The donation list provides an interesting insight into the priorities and terminologies of the time:

- £10 to the Old People's Home, Surbiton
- £8 to the Kingston & District Tuberculosis Care Committee
- £8 to the Society for Spastic Children
- £8 to the Church of England, Childrens' Homes
- £5 to a Leprosy Charity.

1956 The school took over new sports field at Pine Gardens and the first sports day was held there in July. In the girls' sports Raeburn House won followed by Faraday, Elgar and Tennyson. Tennyson won the boys' sports followed by Faraday, Raeburn and Elgar Houses. By 1960 the school was using King George's Recreation Ground for its sports day.

1956 September 3 was Lt. Colonel Hill's last day at the school before he retired. He was replaced by Mr O.C Humphreys BA.

1956 November -1959 September. The school log book was not kept.

1959 The summer exam results showed 3 A level Art passes – unusual for a Secondary Modern School - and a 62% overall pass rate at O level – good, but not many pupils were entered.

1959 October. Two temporary classrooms were added to the school to cope with increasing numbers of pupils. The heating came later!

1959 October. The annual Speech Day was held at the Coronation Hall and the school song "Gratitude" was sung for the first time.

1960 The threat of re-organisation was present as Mr Humphreys attended a meeting regarding the "Surrey Plan".

1961 The old students' events which had run since the time of Mr Hill were still popular with 100 old students attending a dinner in May and the previous headmaster, Mr Hill, was named as a special guest. The end of term was busy time with a prefect and staff party, a choir outing to Penshurst, the PTA fete, a swimming gala at Surbiton Lagoon, and the house dance festival in which 270 girls participated.

1961 September. The pupil roll was now up to 735 causing a serious strain on accommodation and 10 new members of staff started replacing the 7 who left the previous July.

David Forward

1961 December. The Christmas concert was postponed because of smog.

1962 February. The Hollyfield Book club was formed under the guidance of Miss Wood (Anne Wood – later to be of TellyTubbies fame). Later in the year the first film society was established by Mr Davies, Miss Wood with Mr Kedge being the cinematographer. A committee of fifth years formed to help run the society and select the films for showing.

1962 March. The open day for parents was held in the afternoon and evening. This is the first reference to such an event in the school log.

1962 July. The PTA Summer Fair raised a record £260 of which £50 was given to the local "Freedom from Hunger" campaign and over £200 given to the headmaster for the purchase of school equipment.

1963 February. The school was surviving the worst winter since 1947. It was so cold, with snow on the ground from boxing day to early March, that the Thames was frozen over at Kingston and people could walk across the river.

1963 February. The headmaster leads a party of 25 pupils on a tour of Greece.

1963 June. The first full cohort of pupils take "O" level examinations.

1963 An arson attack by a pupil severely damages the school hall. Assemblies etc are moved to the British Legion hall in Hollyfield Road (the dining hall) whilst the school hall is repaired and refurbished. As the hall was also the gymnasium, PE lessons were moved outdoors in the cold much to the disappointment of many of the pupils.

1963 Wimbledon win the Amateur Cup Final at Wembley.

1963 The last main entry in the school log apart from an additional entry by Brigadier Butters, the Chairman of Governors, in May 1965, which noted the change of education authority from Surrey to Kingston upon Thames.

1965 July. The Summer Fair raised £446 13s 6d, most of which was given to the school towards a library for the new school up at Surbiton Hill Road.

1965 September. The Certificate in Secondary Education (CSE) examination was introduced. It was generally for pupils who were likely to fail at GCE O level. A CSE top grade, grade 1, was regarded as equivalent to a basic pass at O level.

1965 November. The prize giving was addressed by Mr JS Bishop the Chief Education Officer for Kingston upon Thames. Two pupils, John Matthews and Robert Cuell, were rewarded for obtaining 8 GCE O level passes.

1966 July. The school leaves the premises in Hollyfield Road in July and moves to the new site on Surbiton Hill in September. The site had been vacated by Surbiton County Grammar School for Boys who had moved to new premises out at Walton on Thames - later to become Esher College.
Mr FA Lamb retired after teaching at the school throughout its time in Hollyfield Road.

1967 September. The school's second year at Surbiton Hill began with 650 pupils on roll.

1967 November. Dame Sybil Thorndyke was the guest of honour at the Prize Giving in the Coronation Hall in Kingston. She received a standing ovation for her speech.

1968 July. The summer fair raised over £800 for the school and its charity, the "Spastics Society". The furthest balloon in the balloon race reached Bagneux in France and the climax of the afternoon was a very realistic demonstration of casualty clearance under battle conditions by the 221 Field Dressing Station, RAMC, from Kingston. The Band of 328 Squadron, Kingston, Air Training Corps provided the music. The Borough Dance Festival was held at Hollyfield soon after and attracted over 500 participants from local schools under the expert eye of Miss Nora Byrne.

1968 During the summer holidays Mrs D.G.J. Head, the school secretary, died. She had been ill for a while and would have been sorely missed as she was a significant support to Mr Humphreys and had been with the school since the war, starting off by working in the canteen at Hollyfield Road before moving with the school up to Surbiton Hill Road in 1966. Pupils attended a memorial service for her.

1969 December. Mr Humphreys gets married for the second time. The school choir sang and formed a guard of honour at his wedding in

Beckenham.

1972 July. Olsen Humphreys retires, aged 65, after serving as Headmaster for 16 years and overseeing the relocation of the school from Hollyfield Road to Surbiton Hill Road.

1972 September. Mr Annets becomes the third substantive Headmaster of the school.

1973 September. The school leaving age was raised to 16 years of age. Known as RoSLA, this initiative spawned a massive building programme, often of dubious standard, as additional classrooms were required across the country. Hollyfield had Olsen House built and named after its previous headmaster Olsen Humphreys. It was a wood framed brick faced building with a flat and leaky roof but gave the school two science laboratories upstairs and three rather cramped general purpose teaching rooms downstairs.

1976 July. Mr Annets leaves after being headmaster for four years.

1976 September. Mrs Joyce Culver becomes acting headteacher for the autumn term.

1977 January. Mr Iowerth Harries becomes the fourth substantive Hollyfield headteacher.

1977 November. Mrs Joyce Culver, previously Deputy Headmistress and Acting Headteacher prior to the appointment of Mr Harries, dies. The school was closed for a day for her memorial service.

1978 November. The Christmas Fair raised £1300.

1979 September. For the first time, pupils in the fourth form (now year 10) take a full range of "Options" through to GCE O level or CSE exams.

1979 October. The first Hollyvine magazine edited by Miss Hendy (later Mrs Huckle)

1979 November. The Christmas Fair target was £1200, "a mammoth target", towards the new school library - £1500 was raised. Male teachers baked cakes for the cake sale with Mr O'Neill's hedgehog cake winning the teachers' prize.

1979 November. New Society published an article about good schools in which they described schools in Kingston by saying ….."some of the secondary moderns are very much better than others. One of the

Hollyfield

better ones is Hollyfield."

1980 May. The first May Fayre was organised by Mrs Hendy (now Huckle) with the tug of war managed by Mr Smith and the 3-legged race overseen by Mr Forward. There was also maypole dancing and several stalls. Stocks with wet sponges were thrown at selected pupils and caused much entertainment. The fayre also ran in 1981, 1982 and 1983.

The Hollyvine pocket money survey concluded the average to be £1.02 per week.

1980 September. A school dinner cost 30p.

1981 February. Hollyfield gets its first computer. It didn't work very well, mainly due to a poor link to the Kingston Polytechnic mainframe which served it. It was replaced in December 1981 by a Research Machine 380Z which included a text editor!

The school's first computer caused great excitement in 1981 – until it was found out that you needed a degree in computer science to work it!
Source: Hollyvine

1981 April. A pupil survey showed pupils' favourite TV programmes to be Grange Hill followed by The Professionals and Top of the Pops. Crossroads was the most disliked.

1981 July. Miss Randall retires from her post as teacher of Commercial Subjects and latterly as Head of Lower School. She is to date the longest serving member of staff having taught at the school from 1947 to 1981, a total of 34 years. She is also distinguished by serving under all the first four Headmasters of the school.

1981 September. The school now had 3 computers, all Sinclair ZX81's with low resolution television screens.

1981 October. The Hollyfield Cookbook was published with a print run of 500 copies which were initially sold by the PTA for a few years and then the rest were given away.

1981 November. The Christmas fair raised £1740 for the school.

1981 December. Over 300 Christmas baskets were delivered to old people by over 600 students. The school received many letters of gratitude.

1982 April. A trip to Russia was bravely run by Mr Cope and Mrs Hendy. Pupils and staff visited both Leningrad and Moscow.

1982 May. After a long wait, the new library opens in the ground floor of Olsen House. It had moved from Albury room A5 which had become too small and was opened by the actor Robin Bailey.

1982 June. Hollyfield holds its first book week with exhibitions, demonstrations on pottery and antiques, storytelling and competitions.

1983 April. The school youth club begins on friday evenings based mainly in the cafeteria and the playground outside. It was run by members of the PTA and Mrs Serbutt the Deputy Head.

1983 Snowy White, the musician visited the school and did an interview for Hollyvine.

1983 The school still had its own sailing boats on the Thames. These were managed by Mr Peter Thorning the Head of Physical Education and a fanatical sailor.
The re-born PTA, known as the HSA (Hollyfield School Association), were running highly successful car boot sales on

Sunday mornings. These filled the large corner playground and visitors jammed up the local roads with their parking.

1983 Eight BBC computers arrived. The school prospectus stated "We feel that computers at Hollyfield will soon be as much as part of life as the blackboard"

1984 February. The school was named by Kingston Local Education Authority as one considered for closure due to falling rolls across the Borough. A packed meeting in the school hall established a campaign which, according to the Surrey Comet, threatened to wage a "bloody battle" against any plan to close Hollyfield. This campaign, led by Declan Terry the PTA chair, whilst not bloody, was strong enough to convince the Authority not to close Hollyfield but unfortunately this led to the closure of Tudor School in North Kingston two years later.

1984 Richard Tracey, member of parliament for Kingston, visited the school twice in the Autumn Term, the second time as the speaker at Certificate Evening in December.

1985 The school now boasted over 20 BBC computers. Computer Studies was becoming a popular Year 10 course.

1985 September. The new Year 10 TVEI (Technical and Vocational Educational Initiative) courses began. These were led by the headmaster, Iowerth Harries who was seconded full time from Hollyfield to the Local Education Authority to lead it. Mrs Eileen Serbutt became Acting Headteacher and Mr David Forward took on her previous role when he was appointed as Acting Deputy Headteacher.

1986 Corporal punishment was abolished in State Schools.

1986 Two new units came into existence – the Special Skills Unit, later to become Special Educational Needs SEN under Mrs Myra Usher, and the Dyslexic Unit or Special Skills Unit under Mrs Shirley Street. This complemented the already existing Hearing Impaired Unit. Each unit could take up to 12 pupils.

1986 April On its third anniversary, the youth club switched on its new floodlights, sponsored by the Sports Council, in the playground known to most as "the cage". The lights were switched on by the then Sports Minister and local MP, Richard Tracey.

1986 – 1988 Monthly Sunday car boot sales continued to be run by the PTA. They were very popular with locals and raised a substantial amount of money for the school.

1986 July. Two ex-pupils try to swim the river Thames at Kingston in the summer after their exams. One, Roy Cooper, drowns.

1986 Summer. The last Hollyvine was printed. There are 28 issues in the school archive from October 1979 to Summer 1986. There was a publication gap until December 1990 when a new newspaper type magazine called " Break – The Voice of Hollyfield" came into existence. Published by an external printer, the front page of the first edition was dominated by "Bike theft on the increase" and a picture of the old bike sheds, which were then fully in sight from Lamberts Road and frequently the target of thieves. "Break" has 7 publications in the school archives running from Dec 1990 to April 1993.

1986 December. The school has its first training day in preparation for the new GCSE's.

1987 January. The school closed for 5 days due to exceptionally heavy snow.

1987 On 23 May it was the 50th anniversary of the school. As this date was in the half term holiday it was not celebrated at this time.

1987 July. A golden jubilee dinner was held with the principal guests being The Mayor, Mrs Jenny Philpott, also a parent of a pupil in the school, and Hollyfield's popular ex-headteacher, Olsen Humphreys. This was Mr Humphreys last visit to the school.

1987 September. Mrs Serbutt becomes the substantive headteacher as Mr Harries' secondment to the Local Education Authority as TVEI Co-ordinator becomes permanent. Mr Forward is confirmed as one of the three permanent Deputy Heads. The maroon blazer is replaced with a black one which is cheaper and more easily obtainable, a move generally welcomed by both pupils and parents. The maroon jumper remained as part of the uniform until July 1991.

1987 September. GCSEs start being taught as a replacement for O levels and CSE exams. Schools received specific grants for in-service education and training (INSET) and new training days, called "Baker Days" after the minister of education who implemented

Hollyfield

them, were introduced.

1987 December. The Certificate Evening speaker was Harvey Burd, an ex –pupil who had risen to the status of an Oxford Professor.

1988 May. Wimbledon beat Liverpool 1 -0 to win the FA Cup final at Wembley.

1988 June. The first of the new GCSE examinations were taken.

1988 September. Lowest ever entry to year 1 of the school. Only 96 pupils joined causing the school roll to fall to a low point of 733. Spanish was offered as a third language for the first time.

1988 October. Cedars House was officially opened on 17 October by Angela Rumbold, Minister of State for Education with the mayor, Councillor Marjorie Hartfree and the local MP Richard Tracey, also present.

1989 May. The first ever Governors' Meeting for Parents was held. This was an annual requirement for governing bodies which now had to report directly to parents. These annual meetings carried on until the last one in November 2005 after which, as it was no longer a legal requirement, they ceased.

1989 July. Hollyfield holds its first Record of Achievement (RoA) evening. The school piloted RoA's ready for a national launch in 1990. Cynically labelled by some as the "Burgundy Wine List" due to its appearance in a maroon thick carded cover it listed all the achievement of pupils throughout their time in school and was given a positive reception by many pupils and their proud parents. The photograph in the Surrey Comet showed Rachel Hutson, Sarah Giordano, Michael Morant, Brian Davis and Bruno Johnson with their RoA files.

1989 September. The new National Curriculum started to be introduced. It began with the first form and worked its way up through the school year on year. Also, the school developed and introduced its own Pastoral Curriculum with a "Form Period" every week. This later evolved into PSHE (Personal, Social and Health Education) lessons. All schools started being responsible for their own budgets under local Management of Schools (LMS). Acronyms were prevalent!

1989 November. A fourth year boy, Tat Whalley, made press headlines in the Surrey Comet for his acting ability. Having performed well in the school production of Oliver he joined a drama group out of school and progressed rapidly to appear in several television shows including Rumpole of The Bailey, Dramarama, The Gift and, A Taste of Death. He also appeared in the film Queen of Hearts. Tat has continued his acting career and is frequently seen on television in a range of programmes including Minder, The Bill and Casualty.

1990 February. Information and Communications Technology (ICT) was beginning to become a more significant subject in the school and this was acknowledged by the national Guardian newspaper which did a substantial piece on ICT courses for teachers with an interview and a picture of Mr Forward.

1990 September. The school renamed the years 1-5 as 7-11 in line with the national curriculum stages. This meant that the first year was now called year 7 and so on.

The school population had reduced to 792 due to a fall in the birth rate and a lessening in the popularity of the school perhaps due to an ongoing loss of confidence in the future of the school following the Local Authority's consultation on school closure a few years earlier. The promotion of the three education support units, which figured prominently in the prospectuses of previous years, was absent from the 1990 prospectus possibly reflecting a view that the school had previously marketed itself differently from the expectations of the majority of local parents.

1990 May. Hollyfield wins the Borough Environmental Pride award (and again in 1991). Some pupils plus Mr Vockings met Princess Alexandra at the signing of Kingston's environmental charter.

1990 December. The Christmas Fair raised £2000.

1991 March. Hollyfield supports the first Comic Relief Day with fund raising activities and events throughout the day.

1991 March. Carol Vorderman visits the school and runs a televised numeracy session.

1991 July. The first ever Hollyfield Activities Day was held. This was deemed so successful that there were 3 days of activities the following year. This was found to be too hard to organise and so it reduced to 2 days for the following few years.

1991 October. Helen Sharman visits to speak to the Year 7 about her career and what it was like being the first British astronaut. She lived locally but then moved to Russia after she married a Russian cosmonaut.

1991 November. The Christmas Fair raised £2500.

1991 September. Much to the delight of most parents and pupils the last vestiges of the maroon uniform disappeared with the replacement of the maroon jumper by a black one.

1991 October. The Library re-opened as Learning Resource centre.

1992 January. The Band of the Coldstream Guards visits and some 15 Hollyfield musicians played with them.

1992 January. The school census shows the low roll of 686 pupils. This is mainly due to the effect of the previous uncertainty over the future of the school. The senior management, staff and governers had to dig deep to maintain positivity and to prove that the school really did provide a good education for local children. This slowly began to have an impact as the following events show.

1992 April. Helen Sharman, the first British astronaut, opens the newly renamed Sharman House, formerly Villiers house. A signed copy of the programme is in the school archives. The re-naming occurred because all the Science laboratories had been refurbished and the corridors re-aligned with a new side entrance and more preparation space for the technicians. A plaque inside the entrance of Sharman commemorates this.

1992 May. May Fair – again the tug of war proved the most popular event.

1992 May. The refurbished technology suite was opened by Lady Parkes.

1992 July. Hollyfield wins the nationally prestigious "Schools' Curriculum Award" based on its excellent community links which was well promoted by the pupils and Mr Vockings. The school celebrated by holding a special lunchtime party on 2 July with Mufti, parties, a large celebration cake, a barbeque and an early closure. David Conway and his Year 11 rock band provided the entertainment.

1992 September. The Office for Standards in Education (Ofsted) was introduced. It was another three years before Hollyfield was inspected.

1992 September. Nearby Kingston Polytechnic was elevated to university status.

1992 October. Hollyfield was a finalist in the prestigious Daily Telegraph school newspaper competition.

1992 November. The Conservatives published plans to set up a third Grammar School in Kingston. This was in response to the application of the Greenwich Judgement of 1989 which stated that schools could not favour children in that LEA over any other LEA in regard to school admissions. This meant that the Kingston Grammar Schools were open equally to all and the effect was that less Kingston pupils were granted entry to them so upsetting a vociferous minority of Kingston parents. A third grammar School would have further reduced the number of able children applying to Hollyfield and Kingston's other non-selective secondary schools and so was a real threat to the improvement the school was making. Fortunately the scheme was seen more as political posturing than a practical reality and was rejected in March 1993.

1993 January. The school heard that it was successful in winning a £200,000 Technology Schools' initiative (TSI) Grant after a lengthy bid process overseen by Mr Forward and Mr Chandler.

1993 April. BBC cameras hit the school at budget time as it was in Chancellor of the Exchequer, Norman Lamont's constituency. The programme they created included clips from Mr Forward's assembly and a follow up interview with him and some Sixth formers about their expectations of the budget. It was shown that evening on the main BBC news.

1993 May. Hollyfield sets up its first counselling service called Face2Face. It was run by an ex-pupil, Paul Sanderson, and intended primarily for the support and counselling of pupils who felt that they were being bullied at school. Paul and his family relocated to Littlehampton in 1996 where Paul led The Wire project which involved supporting young people with caring responsibilities, on behalf of West Sussex County Council Children and Young People's Service. He received an MBE for this work in 2006.

1993 July. Mrs Serbutt leaves after being Headteacher since 1985.

1993 September. Mr Forward becomes Acting Headteacher for the first term of the year. During this time the new school behaviour code is launched.

1993 November. The school begins to spend its award under the Technology Schools Initiative Grant. This grant was used to purchase computers and technology equipment and began many years of technology being a lead subject at the school culminating in it becoming a Technology Specialist School ten years later in 2003.

1994 January. Mr Chamberlain joins as Headteacher. Another tier of management is created with Heads of Upper School and Lower School appointed. Mr Chamberlain watched every teacher teach within his first term.

1994 May. The first Standard Attainment Tasks (SATS) were sat by every pupil in Year 9, the end of Key Stage 3 of the National Curriculum. These lasted until the last ones were taken in May 2008 and led to criticisms in some quarters of denying the fun of childhood as this generation of children were said to be the most tested ever.

1994 December. The last Christmas Fair was held after running annually since the 1970s. It had gradually lost popularity and was no longer a cost-effective way for the PTA to generate funds for the school.

1995 March. The school has its first Ofsted inspection and came out of it with a number of positive comments particularly about the tone and friendliness of the school.

1995 September. The Governing Body voted to recommend that parents vote for the school to apply to the Secretary of State for Grant Maintained (GM) status. This, despite some strong opposition from a minority of parents and others, was followed by a successful ballot of parents in November. The school then had the rest of the academic year to plan for its separation from the Local Education Authority and to appoint auditors, banks etc and to set up contracts with a range of service providers.

1996 July. GM Incorporation Day ie the day Hollyfield officially became a Grant Maintained School.

1996 September. A new school day, based on 6 x 50 minute lessons and ending at 3.20pm, was introduced.

1997 September. In seeking to keep moving forward under its new GM status the school changed its name to The Hollyfield School. The school employed its first former pupil at the Surbiton Hill site when Stewart Duncan was appointed as ICT Technician.

1998 September. Visit to the school by The Right Honorable William Hague MP, leader of the opposition. He met pupils and Mr Chamberlain, dropped in on Drama and Languages lessons and visited the ICT department.

1997 October. The school prospectus now contained a booklet and a summary pamphlet in it. The cover has colour photos on the outside and the inside.

1998 September. The first group of "fast track" pupils started in Year 7 and were selected through the Borough's 11+ test. This was all part of the image improvement by the school and, partly assisted by this change, the school roll jumped from 686 to 753.

1998 October. The school had its second Ofsted inspection which went well for the most part and the inspectors wrote "The school promotes a steady improvement in the results of national tests and public examinations". It was however critical of some aspects of the running of the sixth form and this was subsequently addressed by the school.

1999 July. The local MP, Mr Edward Davey launched his new web-site to the press using the computer room A5. This attracted the local press and resulted in good publicity for the school and its ICT department led by Mr Wyld.

1999 July. Mr Chamberlain organised the first Hollyfield Garden Party for the parents of prospective new pupils. These then ran annually every July through to 2004 and were always pleasant and well attended events held on a Saturday afternoon with good weather, music, drama and refreshments.

1999 September. The roll was up to 820 demonstrating increased confidence in the school by its parents and the local community. The new school year saw the end of traditional paper based registers as "Bromcom " electronic registers were used for both form and lesson registration. Every teacher had to carry around one of the grey mini-laptop type devices. Pupils knew they were being tracked every lesson.

1999 October. Kingston School inspectorate wrote "The school most notably improving GCSE standards over the period 1996 – 1999 is Hollyfield".

1999 November. The school suspends its timetable and holds it first "Target Setting" day. This later became "Academic Guidance" and pupils were tracked on their targets three times a year through appointments with their parents and their form tutors.

1999 November. The newly created Music Technology room was opened by a member of "Blur". Hollyfield with Mr Lennon, was one of the first schools in the country to run an A level in this subject.

2000 January. Hollyfield featured in a substantial article on teachers and laptops in the Times Educational Supplement (TES). The article reported the school's use of Bromcom computers for registration and included a large photo of staff members Mr Shaun Escott, Miss Catherine Anderson, Mr David Forward, Mr Steve Pickett and Mrs Denise Strong on the stairs in Albury House, holding their computers.

2000 February. Following the comments on the Sixth Form by Ofsted in the 1998 inspection and poor post -16 recruitment, Hollyfield joined with Chessington Community College and Southborough Boys' School to form a joint sixth form. Known as "The Kings Collegiate", it was launched in February and the first joint courses with minibus transport between the schools started in September 2000. Its first, and only, Director was Linda Hamer and it ran until July 2004 when Hollyfield pulled out as its Sixth Form was starting to grow again due to the school's increased popularity.

2001 September. Due to its expansion to 961 students as well as natural staff turnover, 14 new staff joined the school. The old maths huts were removed from the back of Albury as work on the new Maths block began.

2001 October. The school received a prestigious award from the Department for Education for being one of the most improved schools in the country. The 5 A★-C GCSE results had gone up from 30% in 1996 to 46% in five years.

2002 September. Oak House, the new Maths block, with six dedicated Maths rooms plus offices was opened by Edward Davey MP for

Kingston upon Thames. The block was modelled on Albury House as it was adjacent to it.

2002 November. Electronic assessments were introduced for the first time using the "Bromcom" laptops. This allowed parents to receive three progress reports a year which were then linked to the target setting days.

2003 March. The school submitted its bid to the Department for Education and Science (DfES) to become a Specialist School for Technology.

2003 July. The first "Sports Personality of the Year" was held. This annual event, initiated by Mr Newman, Head of PE, was very popular with pupils and parents.

2003 September. Improved recruitment meant that the school topped 1000 pupils on roll with 100 in Sixth Form. This further confirmed the improvement of the school from its previous low point.

2003 September. Following its successful bid the school began its new status as a Technology Specialist School which brought in extra capital and revenue funding and was a major boost for the school. Mr Newton, who was also the Head of Maths, was the Director.

2004 February. The school received its third Ofsted inspection. It was over 5 years since the last one. It went smoothly and the school received a good report even though the ICT rooms were in the middle of a complete refurbishment.

2004 March. The school runs its first "HollyTech Day". This popular event run by Mr Forward and Mr Newton, put on activities for primary school pupils from Year 5 and 6 and was run as part of the school's technology college community programme.

2004 May. The school achieved the Football Association Charter Standard for Schools.

2004 August. Whilst on a holiday with friends a popular 15 year old pupil, Matthew Lennon was pulled unconscious from Lake Constance near the German/Swiss border. He died on August 13 in St George's hospital in Tooting having never regained consciousness. He was the son of Clifford Lennon, Assistant Headteacher at the school, and Sally-Ann Lennon a former Hollyfield pupil. The whole school mourned, flowers were laid on the lawns by the cedar trees and the funeral, held in St Mark's Church was full to capacity.

2005 February. Olsen Humphreys, who was the second headmaster of the school and who took the school from Hollyfield Road up to its current site on Surbiton Hill Road, died aged 98. He was headmaster from 1956 until 1972 when he retired.

2005 March. Work started on the new Multi-User Games Area (MUGA) and the long overdue refurbishment of the Gym changing rooms. The MUGA was built on the staff car park which relocated to the back lawn of Albury. To achieve this, a short connecting roadway was built around the back of the Hall with a ramp down to the lawn. The lawn soon became a mud-pit and as some cars became stuck, several layers of gravel had to be added to make it serviceable as a car park.

2005 September. The school roll reached 1032 with 150 in the Sixth Form. The first three study supervisors were employed to cover lessons for absent teachers. Hollyfield was ahead of most schools with this initiative and although unsure about how it would work it proved a success and more study supervisors and a senior study supervisor who arranged the cover were appointed in due course.

Using the extra Technology College money the school was able to provide every teacher with a laptop and equip every room with a digital projector. This further promoted Hollyfield as a centre of excellence for ICT and pupils really appreciated the improvement in lesson quality. The laptops were also used for registration and assessment.

Work was taking place to remove a slice of the large playground adjacent to Lamberts Road and to improve the traffic flow at the Lamberts Road, Surbiton Hill Road, Ewell Road and St Mark's Hill junction. Although slowed down by problems with the railway bridge widening, the resulting landscaping was a major improvement to the junction view of the school.

2006 January. The science department ran its first trip to Euro-Disney. Using data-logging vests they rode the roller coasters and logged the g-forces they generated. This was a very popular trip!

2006 February/March. The school extra-curricular activities were at an all time high. Trips abroad, in these two months alone, included a Battlefields Tour to France and Belgium for Y11,12 & 13; a skiing trip to Italy for Year 8 & 9; a Philosophy Trip to Athens for Y12 & 13; and a Drama trip to New York for Year 12 & 13.

2006 July. Work began on a large extension to Sharman House to be called "New Sharman". The old English hut was demolished and boarding put up around the site. The new building filled in the L shape of old Sharman (formerly Villiers House) and added wide corridors, a sixth form centre on the second floor to house the growing numbers, more ICT rooms on the first floor and a new large Learning Resource Centre on the ground floor to replace the small one in Olsen House.

2006 September. Another ex-pupil joined the staff as Sarah Leighton was employed as one of a growing number of teaching assistants. The pupil roll was up to 1049.

2007 January. Although the school's 5 A*-C GCSE pass rate was up to 61% it was still aiming for further improvement. Mr Chamberlain introduced the "Going for Gold" scheme (G4G) for borderline year 11 students. This used mentor motivator staff as well as extra lessons and proved a great success with results increasing to 73% in 2008 and 82% in 2009.

2007 January. The first "Hollyfit Week" was run by Mr Dan Newman and the PE staff. The Surrey Comet described it in their article as an event to "encourage aspects of good health" and accompanied their report with a photograph of pupils Linda Randall and Claire Ferris and others exercising in the gymnasium. Sports events were held throughout the week and in most years culminated in a staff v pupils football match on the Friday lunchtime which the staff nearly always won whilst the spectating pupils enjoyed the amusement.

2007 September. Another ex-pupil joined the school staff. Miss Claire Briggs was employed as a graduate trainee art teacher.

2008 February. Ofsted inspected for the fourth time and after a two day visit categorised the school as a "good" school with an "outstanding" being awarded for contribution to the community which included extra-curricular activities and the broader curriculum.

2008 April. The PTA held a very successful "Auction of Promises" which raised over £3000 towards the installation of a £40,000 double canopy, known as "The Dome" in the play area between the Music block and Sharman House. This impressive structure quickly became a popular meeting and eating place for pupils.

2008 May. The school was the first secondary school in Kingston Local Authority to be awarded the national ICT Mark for excellence in its ICT provision.

2008 September. New Sharman was gradually brought into use. It took two years to build as the initial contractor went into liquidation part way through construction causing delay whilst a new contractor was found and whilst they orientated to the contract. The new building with its glass front and modern rooms was a great addition to the school and a major improvement for the sixth form who occupied the top floor.

2009. Hollyfield was recognised by the Specialist School and Academies Trust (SSAT) as one of the most improved schools in the country for that year as it had improved its 5 A★-C GCSE rate by more than 10% between 2007 and 2008.

2009 August. The GCSE 5A★-C pass rate reached 80% (63% including English and Maths) with a 97% A level pass rate (669.7 average points score per student). This was the best ever year for academic results and showed that the school had come a long way since 1996 when it only achieved 30% 5A★-C GCSE passes.

2009 November. The school is notified that it will receive a new building programme BSF (Building Schools for the Future) worth about £20 million. The aim is to develop the site substantially and remove all the huts and other unsuitable buildings. To cope with a surge in the birth rate, it is suggested that the school might possible expand to 8 forms of entry, an increase of 60 pupils in each year.

2010 May. The national election result with the new coalition government looking at the budget deficit causes a halt in the capital building programme and puts the BSF project at risk.

2010 July. It seems certain that the national financial situation will affect education, possibly with schools in supposedly more affluent areas like Kingston being most badly affected. One new opportunity presented is that of "Academy" status with direct funding and this is being considered by the school and the Governing Body.

David Forward

Famous Staff

Anne Wood (1960 -1965)

Anne Wood taught English at Hollyfield Road from 1960 -1965. It was her second job, having previously taught in Durham, and she recalls that she "had to modify my 'Geordie' accent to meet the expectations of the pupils". She was a popular teacher who left in 1965 to go into children's publishing and this led to some TV work. Her skills were clearly recognised as in 1981, she became the Head of children's programming on TV-am. In 1984 she founded "Ragdoll" and has continued as its creative director to the present day. Ragdoll is based in Stratford-upon-Avon and has produced "Pob's Programme", "Brum", "Rosie and Jim", "Tot's TV", "Teletubbies", "Boobah" and "In the Night Garden", which won a BAFTA Children's award in 2007 as well as the best Pre-School Programme Award at the Broadcast Awards in 2010. Ragdoll has also supported and sponsored a number of organisations and activities for disabled and disadvantaged children.

As a consequence of her media and charitable work Anne has been the recipient of a number of prestigious awards including, in 2000, the CBE for services to children's broadcasting. Other awards include; the Eleanor Farjeon Award for services to children's books (1969); the Roland Politzer Award for book promotion (1974); the Veuve Clicquot Award for business woman of the year (1998); a Bafta special award, for outstanding contribution to children's TV (2000); and the Olswang Business Award (2003), presented by Five/Women in Film & Television.

Referring to her time at Hollyfield Road, Anne says that the school was run on traditional, rather strict lines but that she loved teaching English there. She says: "There were some great pupils many of whom were well up to taking, in those days, their GCEs. I loved teaching them and enjoyed their success. I especially liked it because we could all have ambition to achieve a real goal."

Anne also remembers that she enjoyed teaching drama, putting on film shows for the older pupils and taking school trips to the theatre:

"We had one particularly talented boy, Christopher Wren, who performed in my production of 'Young Visitors' who also played music for big old silent films e.g. 'The General' by Buster Keaton."

Geoffrey Miller (1959-1964) was a pupil who really appreciated Anne's teaching: He says:

"I have very fond memories of Anne Wood, who took me for English for my last two years. She was the person who thought that I had some sort of problem and that I wasn't just a thick thug. She was right because I don't think the word Dyslexia had been invented then but many years later this came to light for me."

Anne was also a form teacher, something she also enjoyed. She says: "It gave the opportunity to understand the personalities of the pupils and believe me there were some personalities!!" Leo Whisstock (1961 – 1966) was a pupil in Anne's form (1A) in 1961/2 when he started at Hollyfield Road but recalls: "She left a couple of years after to go into the book world (she started the book club at the school while I was in her class). She was often to be seen on TV on book programmes etc. and then later on I saw a bit of an awards programme and they showed Anne in the audience and mentioned that she was the one behind the Teletubbies."

Anne's enthusiasm was clear and she says:

" I suppose my over riding passion while at Hollyfield Road was that children should expand their horizons through reading and it is to the credit of the school that I was given every opportunity to do whatever experimental work that occurred to me to spread that enthusiasm."

A particular play Anne remembers was "George and the Dragon", produced with first and second formers for a school open day. She also recalls starting a paper back book club through what became the Scholastic Paper Book Scheme. Apparently, it was one of the first in the UK, and it led indirectly to her opportunity to work in children's publishing. She has always been surprised that starting a school book club in a non-selective secondary school in Surbiton could lead to such great things. This seems to confirm that it was probably more the person than the activity which led to such a great career in the media and philanthropy.

Famous Pupils

Tony "Duster" Bennett 1957 – 1962

Tony was one of the first famous blues performers to come out of Hollyfield. In addition to school, Tony was also a Sea Scout and attended the Leander group on the River Thames at Kingston where he also knew a fellow Hollyfield pupil, Anthony Topham. Although they were only vague friends at this time, their friendship increased greatly after they left school as they shared an exceptional musical ability which later connected formally through the Yardbirds.

Like many others, Tony went from the school to Kingston Art College but his talent at music always exceeded his talent at pottery and he was signed up by the Swan Song record label in 1975. Sadly, it was a career cut short in 1976 when he was only 30 years old. He was driving back from a gig late at night when he probably fell asleep at the wheel of his Ford Transit van and was killed in a collision with a lorry.

His style was country blues, but his method of performing was very individualistic involving him as a one-man-band playing guitar, percussion and harmonica. He wrote many songs, most notably "Jumping at Shadows" which was subsequently covered by Fleetwood Mac and the blues rocker Gary Moore. He also wrote for the Yardbirds and performed with many famous names in Britain, Australia and the US. His biography "Jumping at Shadows" was written by Martin Celmins and published in 2007.

Eric Clapton 1958 - 1961

Eric Clapton is without doubt the most famous and richest of the school's ex-pupils. He was born in March 1945 in Ripley, an attractive Surrey village about half way between Surbiton and Guildford. His mother, Patricia Clapton, was only 16 years old when Eric was born and his father was Edward Fryer, a 24 year old Canadian soldier. His father went off to war before Eric's birth and then returned to Canada.

Eric grew up largely in the care his grandmother, Rose Clapp, and her second husband Jack, and for many years Eric thought that they were his parents and that his mother was actually his older sister. His mother later married another Canadian soldier and moved to Canada with him, leaving Eric totally with what were his grand parents. When he was nine years old, Eric apparently discovered his true family situation when his mother and his six year old half-brother returned to England for a visit. It appears that this was a low experience in his life with the consequence that he stopped applying himself fully at school, became more moody and distanced himself somewhat from his family.

His early schooling was local to Ripley but when Eric was 13 he was awarded an art scholarship to join the specialist art group at Surbiton Central School in Hollyfield Road. This meant that every day from September 1958, he travelled by train up to Surbiton and either went to the school main building in Hollyfield Road or to its art annexe at 35, Ewell Road.

Although talented artistically and musically, it appeared that Eric was still affected by the experiences of his early life. This was observed by his peers at school who described him as rather shy, moody and withdrawn. However, they acknowledged his talent with a guitar and enjoyed his concerts in the hall at Hollyfield Road as well as his informal strumming in the cloakroom at "35" or even in the summer, during lunch breaks, in the Alexandra Recreation Ground opposite the main school. Eric describes himself at this time as a quiet, lonely and "nasty kid", who was very serious about his musical goals. He was also known for his sense of humour, often at the expense of his teachers. Dorothy Lambert (1957 – 1963), who was in Eric's Art group at the school Art Annex at 35 Ewell Road says, "Eric was a great practical joker and I remember he drove one form tutor wild (although she always had a smile on her face) when we were registered in the upstairs domestic science room next to the staff room. The prints of a mysterious one legged man with a crutch appeared all over the work surfaces for several mornings and had us in stitches." Also, "One year we were registered in Mr Cootes' hut and Eric and his pals used to drape themselves over the outside steps and shout "Aiderrrr" (Ada) in a west country accent whenever we ventured within earshot. Ada was the nick name for a girl in our form and this was very funny at the time!"

Eric received an acoustic Spanish Hoya guitar for his 13th birthday, but apparently found learning the instrument very difficult and nearly gave up. Despite his frustrations, he was influenced by "The Blues" from an early age and practised long hours to learn the chords and imitate the famous artists of the day. He was often seen by other pupils of the school, staring intently through the window of Bell's Music shop in the Ewell Road near to "35" and looking enviously at the new colourful electric guitars which were just coming into vogue. Although Eric was in Fifth Art when Anthony "Top" Topham was in Third Art, they soon became musically bound friends and Eric would sometimes go home with Top, whose mum would feed them both. They used to think it was cool to drink coffee and to eat garlic together. Top describes Eric as "dark but bright".

Not much remains of Eric's relatively short time at the school although a copy of a poem he wrote when he was in the Third Year, called "The Battle Cry", was published in the school magazine and reprinted in the 1979 school prospectus. In the school archives there is also a poetry book first issued in 1959 with Eric Clapton's name written inside the front cover in red ink but it is uncertain if this is genuine or not. A contemporary of Eric's at the school, Arthur Knevett, confirms that although Eric was quite a shy person he really enjoyed his art and English. On the basis of his GCE in both these subjects, Eric left Hollyfield in 1961 to go to Kingston College of Art to study stained-glass window making. Unfortunately, he found it hard to settle and was dismissed at the end of the first academic year because his focus remained on his music rather than his art.

In his spare time Eric was concentrating on his guitar-playing and was soon busking around Kingston, playing gigs locally and then in London with a band called the "Roosters". In 1963 he replaced another Hollyfield pupil, Anthony "Top" Topham, in the newly formed "Yardbirds", the blues based band born out of Hollyfield and three of its pupils. As the Yardbirds sound evolved into experimental rock, "For your Love" was a great hit in 1965 which happened to be the time that Eric was leaving them to pursue his passion for Rhythm and Blues. In 1966 he formed "Cream" until their demise in 1968 during which time they had many hits and became internationally famous. He also supported various other bands in the late 1960s.

Eric Clapton's career successes in the 1970s were in stark contrast to his personal life, which, unfortunately, was troubled by romantic longings and drug and alcohol addiction. "I Shot the Sherrif" was Clapton's first Number One hit and was important in bringing reggae and the music of Bob Marley to a wider audience. During an August 1976 concert in Birmingham, Clapton provoked a controversy that has continued to follow him, when he made pointed remarks from the stage in support of Enoch Powell's efforts to restrict immigration to the U.K. His troubled life continued throughout the 1980s with drink and relationship difficulties. He became a born again Christian but this did not protect him from tragedy as in 1990, fellow guitarist Steve Vaughan, who was touring with Clapton, together with two members of their road crew were killed in a helicopter crash between concerts. Then, in 1991, Eric's son Conor, who was four years of age, died when he fell from the 53rd-story window of his mother's friend's New York City apartment, landing on the roof of an adjacent four-story building. Clapton's grief was expressed in the song "Tears in Heaven", which received a total of six Grammys.

Throughout the 1990s and the 2000s Clapton, or "Old Slowhand" as he is known, has continued to play with various bands or performed solos always amazing the crowds with his talent and is widely regarded as one of the greatest rock guitarists of all time as well as a popular singer/song writer. In 2004, he received a CBE from the Princess Royal at Buckingham Palace and in 2006, received the Grammy Lifetime Achievement Award. This is also a great source of pride for the school, which shaped his formative years and gave him the opportunity to develop into such a world class musician.

Chris Dreja 1958 - 1963

Chris was a member of Hollyfield in the late 1950s and early 1960s. He too was a pupil in the Art stream and for several of his lessons had to walk with others up to 35 Ewell Road. His father was polish and Chris soon became an accomplished acoustic guitar player.

Audrey Whyman (1959 – 1963) was in the same class as Chris and says that he was a really nice but rather quiet boy. She recalls that sometimes Chris used to bring his guitar to school and would play quietly in the corner of the room particularly on wet lunchtimes. She also remembers that other pupils used to play along with him. She says "They were not the focus of the room, several classmates would be around them, but there was no "Wow" factor at that time!"

Peter Leckstein (1959 – 1963) also remembers Chris as a brilliant artist as well as a superb guitar player. Chris was persuaded to switch to electric guitar and was a member of a popular group called the Metropolitan Blues Quartet. This band then evolved into the Yardbirds where Chris played with two other ex-Hollyfield musicians, Anthony "Top" Topham and Eric Clapton. He wrote some Yardbirds songs and, although he was later offered a place in what was to become Led Zepplin, he refused in order to pursue a career as a photographer. He was still playing and performing guitar in 2008.

Anthony Topham 1958 – 1963

Anthony "Top" Topham was another talented musician and member of the 35, Ewell Road art group. His parents, particularly his father who was a skilled fine artist as well as a fan of jazz and blues, were so keen for him to join the school's specialist Art stream that they moved house from Hayes, Middlesex, to near the Railway Hotel at Norbiton just so he could attend the Hollyfield Road school. He used to cycle to school from Norbiton even though he used to suffer from asthma.

When he was in his second year, Anthony met Chris Dreja and they became great friends with common interests in Art and Music. During his second year, his artistic talent was obvious and he did two murals for the school, one was a large frieze in Mrs Bradley's Music room and the other on Miss Richbell's Art room wall. At the end of the second year, even though Mr Humphreys had commented on his "slightly unruly behaviour", he was delighted when he was allowed to join the art stream for the next three years. "Top" describes these three years as "magic" and he went on to obtain a distinction in O level art at the end of the fourth year followed by a distiction at A level art in his fifth and final year at the school. Mr Humphreys even had one of Anthony's paintings hanging on his office wall.

Early on "Top" was a skiffle player and badly wanted to play the drums but his parents could not afford to buy him a drumkit. It was only later on, after many hours spent "gawping" in the window of Bells Music shop in the Ewell Road and worrying the shopkeeper, who they called "Drac" because seemed to rise up from behind the counter when customers entered, that he and also Chris Dreja, were able to afford to buy their first guitars from there.

"Top" used to play guitar, with Chris on piano or guitar and sometimes also with his older friend Eric Clapton, at the school in concerts and at lunch times on the days when they attended their Art classes at 35 Ewell Road. The lunch time impromptu gigs were known to others such as senior pupils from the nearby Surbiton County Grammar School, then occupying the current Hollyfield site on

Surbiton Hill, who sometimes went there as they were allowed out of school at lunchtimes. Evening visits to the Railway Hotel, Norbiton, allowed them play time and their version of R & B was well received. "Top" and Chris Dreja, met singer and harmonica player Keith Relf, bassist Paul Samwell-Smith and drummer Jim McCarty and formed a new group called the Yardbirds in May 1963, whilst "Top" was still in his final year at the school.

One of "Tops" favourite bands was newly formed Rolling Stones. He was often present on a Sunday night at the Station Hotel in Richmond when the Stones performed and he became a real fan being especially impressed by the guitar and harmonica playing of Brian Jones. Top says, that when the Yardbirds were formed, they were influenced by the Stones but that the Yardbirds style contained more improvisation. When the Rolling Stones went on tour the Yardbirds became the band at the Crawdaddy Club in Richmond and gained an increased following. This posed a problem for Chris as he would have to turn professional and, with fears about his Art course and apparently some parental disapproval, he left and was replaced by his friend and another Hollyfield pupil, Eric Clapton.

According to Wikipedia, Topham recalls: "I was only 15 then, three or four years younger than the rest, and there was no way my parents would let me go out five or six nights a week to play music, even though I was already bringing home double what my father was earning. I was going on to Epsom Art School and they wanted me to take it seriously. Eric Clapton was the obvious person to replace me."

"Top" went on to Art College where he could not resist forming a new band and later joined Winston G and the Wicked (later renamed The Fox), once again finding himself at a pivotal point in British rock as the band crossed from heavy rock to psychedelia. He played alongside musical greats such as Marc Bolan, Yes and Captain Beefheart. Over the years he played with a number of bands and on several recordings including a solo album for Blue Horizon, "Ascension Heights". During the 1970s and 1980s he left the music scene for a while, converted to Islam, became an interior designer and artist, married and had ten children. He again played with Jim McCarty forming the Top Topham-Jim McCarty Band as well as contributing to many other sessions and recordings. He currently appears on the blues scene on a more occasional basis including with the latest edition of the Yardbirds with Jim McCarty and Chris Dreja.

Top remembers several teachers from the Hollyfield Road school and from 35 Ewell Road. In particular, he remembers liking and learning a lot from Mr Kedge who taught him for a combined course which linked Art, Music and literature which Top found inspirational. He also liked and got on well with, Mr Dyson and Mr Strachan. Although Top describes himself as "hopeless" at Maths, he also had a great respect for Mr Hann who taught him geometry in a very patient way.

Two events which Top remembers well were connected with two teachers, one with Mrs Bradley, the Music teacher and the other with the headmaster, Mr Humphreys. Firstly, Anthony and other pupils watched a solar eclipse from Mrs Bradley's music room window in 1961. After watching it intently he found that his sight was dark. When he went for an eye check up it was confirmed that the solar glare had burned part of his retina and caused permanent damage, a problem which affects him to this day. His memory is also that Mr Humphreys was "very long-suffering " with him but that this changed a few days before he left. This was because Anthony and a few other boys came across a batch of cakes that had been made for one of the end of year functions. The opportunity was too good to miss and they helped themselves to some of the cakes leading to great upset by the staff over the stealing and a caning from Mr Humphreys. Top found this ironic as whilst he was being caned by Mr Humphreys, one of Tops paintings was hanging just above, on Mr Humphreys office wall!

Ken Badger (known professionally as Ken Leray)

Ken wrote "Together We Are Beautiful" a popular single by Fern Kinney. The song reached number one in the UK singles chart for a single week in March 1980. The song was also sung by Ken in the opening episode of the first season of the BBC2 sitcom, Early Doors, whilst his character was carrying out bar/landlord duties. Ken also wrote music for the "Doctor Snuggles" cartoons in the 1970s and 1980s.

Nigel Treherne 1962 – 1967

Nigel was one of the pupils who moved up with the school from Hollyfield Road to Surbiton Hill. He remembers that Mrs Burridge, one of the music teachers, enthused him about Music and was very encouraging to him as he studied for his music O level. He was given special privilege to play his oboe in the Albury "dungeons" during breaks but as there was no GCE music class running he had to come back in the evenings and do his O level as part of the Adult Education classes that the school hosted. Other teachers Nigel particularly remembers were Mr Kedge, English literature, who gave the class a list of 100 books that one had to read during life and Mr Hann, geography, who kindly gave Nigel a set of fossils that he has kept to this day.

Nigel did his A levels at Tiffin School and went on to study oboe, violoncello and composition at the Royal College of Music. He then won a German academic exchange scholarship and this led to a long career as an oboist and composer across many European countries. He has written many works for the musical theatre including two award winning musicals; "Maria" and Paparazzi". He has also written a considerable amount of chamber music including many pieces for his own instrument, the oboe. He works and plays across Europe and lives with his wife in the Black Forest, Germany.

Tat Whalley 1985 – 1990

Tat first made the headlines when on his debut he performed the lead role in the school production of Oliver in 1987. Having been recommended for the part by his Music teacher, Joan Wilson, Tat performed so well that he was encouraged by Hollyfield staff to join a local dramatic group and before long he had acquired an agent and appeared in his first television part in the drama "A Taste for Death "(1988). This was the start of his acting career which has included many TV parts in programmes such as "Rumpole of the Bailey (1989), The Bill (1992 and 2008), Minder (1994), Casualty (1994), A Touch of Frost (1995) and Silent Witness (2010) as well as numerous drama and film appearances.

David Forward

The punishment book

This tatty dull red exercise book with a gummed white label on it with the heading "Punishment book" "Mr Annets" is held in the school archives and holds some fascinating history. It was a requirement for all schools to officially record their use of corporal punishment.

The Hollyfield punishment book was introduced in September 1972 by the then headmaster Mr Annets, with the first entry being in May 1973. The privilege of being the first fell to a third year boy for repeatedly being insolent to a teacher and then walking out of the class. The punishment was "1 on seat" and the entry was initialled by the Headmaster.

The next entry was for what was obviously regarded as a more serious offence as it received "2 on seat". This was to a different pupil for "swinging a chain in the classroom and hitting four children". No further details are given but a major disturbance and some injury were caused. Smoking, rudeness and "deplorable behaviour" also received one hit. Other offences included "letting down the tyres of a member of staff's car", "letting off a stink bomb", "interfering with a girl" as well as truanting and stealing. Most of the entries were for offences such as smoking, disruptive behaviour or foul language especially to female members of staff. Mr Annets always carried out the punishments himself and when he left in 1976, Mr O'Neill took over during the term that Mrs Calver was acting headteacher.

From 1976, it appears that both the administrator of the punishment and also a witness had to sign the punishment book. The punishment at this time was nearly always "2 on seat" with 3 given to two pupils in December 1976 for "explosion wrecking a school desk".

When Mr Harries became the headteacher in September 1977, he too chose to administer the punishments himself. Mr Harries always believed that he should not expect other staff to do things unless he was prepared to do them himself. The punishments were still "2 on seat", with Mr O'Neill, now the deputy head, usually the witness although it was occasionally other staff, always male, such as Mr Vockings, Mr Thorning and Mr Gealy. Usually, there was little or no discussion with the pupil as to why the punishment was being given, merely a statement by Mr Harries about the reason and then, "bend over boy" and whilst the boy bent over, Mr Harries would pick up a bamboo cane secreted nearby, "lower", "lower", thwack, thwack, "stand up boy". The boy was then sent out of the study with the punishment completed and the book then duly filled in and signed by Mr Harries and the witness.

Other offences recorded as receiving corporal punishment included; rocking a teacher's car, forging a teacher's signature, fighting, impersonating a prefect and cheating during exams. Another reason given was "causing a noxious smell". The source was not specified! Spitting and vandalism appear as additional reasons to warrant corporal punishment in the early 1980s, otherwise the reasons given did not vary much until May 1986 when Mrs Serbutt was Acting Headteacher when the final entry was made for "extreme rudeness to a teacher". Mrs Serbutt, the only female member of staff to do so, witnessed two beatings in 1986. Possibly, this was partly the reason why corporal punishment at Hollyfield stopped at this time although it was outlawed nationally in state schools in 1987.

David Forward

Hollyfield Headteachers

Lt. Col FWC Hill	1937-1956
Mr FW Beale	1939-1942 (Acting during War)
Mr H Cleland	1943-1945 (Acting during War)
Mr Olsen Humphreys	1956-1972
Mr Annets	1972-1976
Mrs Joyce Culver	1976 (Acting)
Mr Iowerth Harries	1977-1985 (seconded to Local Authority 85-7)
Mrs Eileen Serbutt	1985-1993 (Acting 85 – 87)
Mr David Forward	1993 (Acting)
Mr Stephen Chamberlain	1994–present

It is both notable and commendable that to date, Hollyfield has only had six substantive Headteachers, shown above in bold, since it was first established in 1937.

Deputy Headteachers

Miss Mabel E Guyer	1937-1949
"Chief Woman Assistant"	
Miss Nora Byrne	1950-1970
Mrs Joyce Culver	1970-1977
Mr Dennis O'Neill	1976-1980
Mrs Serbutt	1978-1985
Promoted to Headteacher	
Mr Jim Forrest	1981-1987
Mr Laurie Smith	1987-1989
Mr John Vockings	1980-1992
Mrs Angela Hepple	1989-1997
Mrs Janice Anastasi	1997-2002
Mr David Forward	1985-2009
Dr Jacqueline Bandara	2009-

As can be ascertained from the dates the number of deputy headteachers varied between one and three depending on the size of the school and the structure of the rest of the senior management team at the time.

David Forward

Long Serving Teachers

Mr FA Lamb (all the time the school was at Hollyfield Road)	1937-1966	29 years
Miss Joan Randall	1947-1981	34 years
Mr Ron Gealy	1957-1990	33 years
Mrs Marian Pinkus (nee Gordon) 22 out of 28 years	1964-67, 1968-69, 1974-92.	
Mr Peter Thorning	1963-1995	33 years
Mr John Phelan	1970-1997	27 years
Mr Frank Carlisle	1972-2005	33 years
Mrs Janet Huckle	1975-	
Mr David Forward	1979-2009	30 years

Also very worthy of mention is Peter Gray, who was first appointed as a Governor of the school in 1974, was chair of the Governing Body in the late 1970s until he became Deputy Mayor of Kingston in 1984/5, and was still continuing as a Governor in 2010.

School Plays

1952	Pussycat, or the Squire of Wensleydale – Miss HM Derbyshire/Mr B Eastland
1954	Three Pills in a Bottle – Miss HM Derbyshire
1960	Jane Eyre -
1962	Bethlehem – Mrs J Bradley/Mrs HM Rudge
1963	David Copperfield – Mr RW Davies
1966	The Gondoliers – Mr RW Davies
1967	The Pirates of Penzance – Mr Lyn Swanson
1968	The Mikado – Mr Lyn Swanson
1970	A Man for All Seasons –
1971	The Real Inspector Hound -
1979	Androcles and the Lion - Mr Laurie Smith, Mrs Salaun
1980	West Side Story - Mr John Vockings
1980	The Thwarting of Baron Bolligrew - Mrs Janet Hendy
1981	Tom Jones - Lyn Swanson
1981	Sweeny Todd - Mr John Vockings, Mrs Serbutt, Mr Smith
1983	Charlie and the Chocolate Factory - Mr Jeremy Davies
1983	Playboy of the Western World - Mr Jeremy Davies
1985	Rock Scenes - Mr Jeremy Davies
1987	Oliver -
1988	Bugsy Malone -
1989	The Dracula Spectacula - Mrs Cathy Hudson
1990	Black Comedy – Mrs Suzanne Gunton
1990	Television - Mrs Cathy Hudson
1991	Grease – Mrs Cathy Hudson
1993	Sweeny Todd - Mrs Cathy Hudson
2001	An Evening of Drama - Miss Marianne O'Shea
2002	The Farndale Avenue Housing Estate Towns Women's Guild Dramatic Society Murder Mystery - Miss Marianne O'Shea
2003	Our Country's Good – Ilex Theatre Company

2004   Road – Ilex Theatre Company
2004   Bugsy Malone – Ilex Theatre Company
2005   Twelfth Night – Ilex Theatre Company
2005   Living with Lady MacBeth – Ilex Theatre Company
2005   Grease – Ilex Theatre Company
2006   Black Comedy –- Ilex Theatre Company
2006   The Importance of Being Earnest – Ilex Theatre Company
2006   Little Shop of Horrors – Ilex Theatre Company
2007   A Midsummer Night's Dream – Ilex Theatre Company
2007   Into the Woods – Ilex Theatre Company
2008   A Thoroughly Modern Millie – Ilex Theatre Company
2009   Crazy for You – Ilex Theatre Company

This is not a complete list and an omission of a year does not mean that a play did not take place merely that the school archives have no record of it. The quality of school plays has always been exceedingly high.

Certificate Evening Speakers

A few examples:
1967   Dame Sybil Thorndike
1979   Miss Auriol Stevens, Observer education correspondent
1981   Mr Baker, retired Kingston inspector
1987   Harvey Burd, Oxford University and an ex-pupil

David Forward

School Inspections

Brought in by the Education Act 1992 which created Ofsted (Office for Standards in Education) and their inspectors. The school had Ofsted inspections in:

1995
1998
2004
2008

Hollyfield

Pupils Who Have Represented Their Country

Kate Saunders	English Schoolgirl Volleyball squad 1980
Michael Dunkley	British Schoolboy weightlifting champion 75 kilo class 1980
Neville Wright	English National Under 14 Hurdles champion
Mohammed Sobihy	Rowing – 2005 on.

David Forward

Head Boys

1948-49		1976-77	C. FRY	2006	JASON DANIELS
1949-50	A. HARPER	1977-78	J. REED	2007	DUANE HARRISON
1950-51	D. WARD	1978-79	H. ROCK	2008	THOMAS WHITE
1951-52	J. FOSTER	1979-80	PAUL CANHAM / ROBERT IVEY		
1952-53	M. HOMES	1981-82	CARL WONFOR		
1953-54	J. COLLEY	1982-83	ROBERT WADDELL		
1954-55	G. VARNDELL	1983	ANDREW HACKMAN		
1955-56	G. VARNDELL	1985	STEVEN HARMAN		
1956-57	B. CRUMP	1986	KEITEL SURI		
1957-58	D. TOFT	1987	ROGER BHATIA / MATTHEW TAYLOR		
1958-59	A. GOODBOURN				
1959-60	D. BOXALL	1988	STUART BALL		
1960-61	D. WALKER	1989	DANIEL BRADFORD		
1961-62	A. MASON	1990	SIMON BRODIE		
1962-63	J. STRAINGE	1991	ANDREW HAMILTON		
1963-64	B. MORRIS	1992	SUNEIL BHATIA		
1964-65	A. STANFORD	1993	JONATHAN COX		
1965-66	D. TUCKNOTT	1994	STEVEN MARTIN		
1966-67	D. MOSS-BOWPITT	1995	CHETAN PATEL		
1967-68	A. PERRETT / M. TAYLOR	1996	JAMES WHITE		
1968-69	C. MARTIN	1997	JAMES GRIGGS		
1969-70	G. POINTS	1998	TOM GIBBS		
1970-71	C. WOOD	1999	TOM JEFFREY		
1971-72	G. MELLON-GRANT	2000	JAMIE ZEQIRI		
1972-73	J. NAISH	2001	NICHOLAS LONG		
1973-74	P. WINDEATT	2002	WILLIAM SHAND		
1974-75	G. SEATON	2003	MARK ROWAN		
1975-76	C. CHILD	2004	SAFWAN AFRIDI		
		2005	SAFWAN AFRIDI		

Hollyfield

Head Girls

HEAD GIRL

1948-49	J. CURTIS
1949-50	P. WEST
1950-51	J. HEATH
1951-52	A. ROGERS
1952-53	M. EDWARDS
1953-54	J. NEEDLE
1954-55	C. ELLIS
1955-56	W. SMITH
1956-57	D. TANNER
1957-58	M. JOSEPH
1958-59	J. DUNBAR
1959-60	J. BLYTH
1960-61	C. RIDGE
1961-62	S. TURNER
1962-63	B. BENNETT
1963-64	S. DAVIES
1964-65	S. HOYTE
1965-66	D. GUBBINS
1966-67	C. FIFIELD
1967-68	J. LANGHORNE
1968-69	J. LANGHORNE
1969-70	R. DANE
1970-71	C. WILLIAMS
1971-72	A. LANE
1972-73	H. BOWDEN
1973-74	R. DRURY
1974-75	A. HEASMAN
1975-76	J. MELLON-GRANT
1976-77	E. CROMBIE
1977-78	K. ROBERTS
1978-79	K. ELLINGER
1979-80	KATE SAUNDERS
1981-82	ELIZABETH KANE
1982-83	PRAKSHA PATEL
1983	ALISON LINTOTT
1985	TANIA HUNTER
1986	JULIE DRAKE
1987	SHARON HARDWICK
1988	DONNA GINN
1989	SHEENA NAGAR
1990	ELEANOR COTTLE
1991	CLAIRE LILLEY
1992	CORINNE BUTLER
1993	LOUISE WATSON
1994	KELLY NAISH
1995	VICTORIA LEWIS
1996	NATALIE ALLEN
1997	LOUISE RAY
1998	MARIA HENDERSON
1999	ANITA VASSA
2000	TERRI SOUSTER
2001	SOPHIE ALEXANDER
2002	HANNAH WILSON
2003	EMMA BURNELL
2004	LAURIE ROWBOTTOM
2005	LAURIE ROWBOTTOM
2006	RACHEL GREEN
2007	GEMMA NAPAUL
2008	POLLY DUNN

Bibliography

Clapton, Eric, 2007; *Clapton: The Autobiography*, Pub: Broadway
Forward, AJ. 1946, *Surbiton County Grammar School; The first Twenty-one Years*.
Hollyfield and *Hollyvine* – the school magazines.
Kingston Borough News 22 September 1972
Kingston Informer 7 May 1993.
Kingston, Surbiton and New Malden Times 30 July 1999.
Leissner, D. 2009; *Hollyfield 1969 – 1973* (unpublished)
Richardson RWC, 1888, *Thirty-Two Years of local self government 1885 – 1887*, Pub: Bull & Son
Statham R, 1996; *Surbiton Past*, Phillimore
Surbiton: The Official Guide, 1928, 1938 and 1947
Surrey Comet 12 December 1936
Surrey Comet 12 December 1977.
Surrey Comet 3 February 1984
Surrey Comet 28 October 1988
Surrey Comet – special Hollyfield News supplement 3 November 1989
Surrey Comet 28 September 1998
Surrey Comet 23 April 2004
Surrey Comet 27 August 2004
Surrey Comet 21 May 2008.
Surrey Education Committee: Log Book for Surbiton Central Mixed School 1937 -1965
The London Gazette 5 May 1939
The Surbitonian: Summer 1959
The Times Educational Supplement 7 January 2000
Wikipedia